POTTED

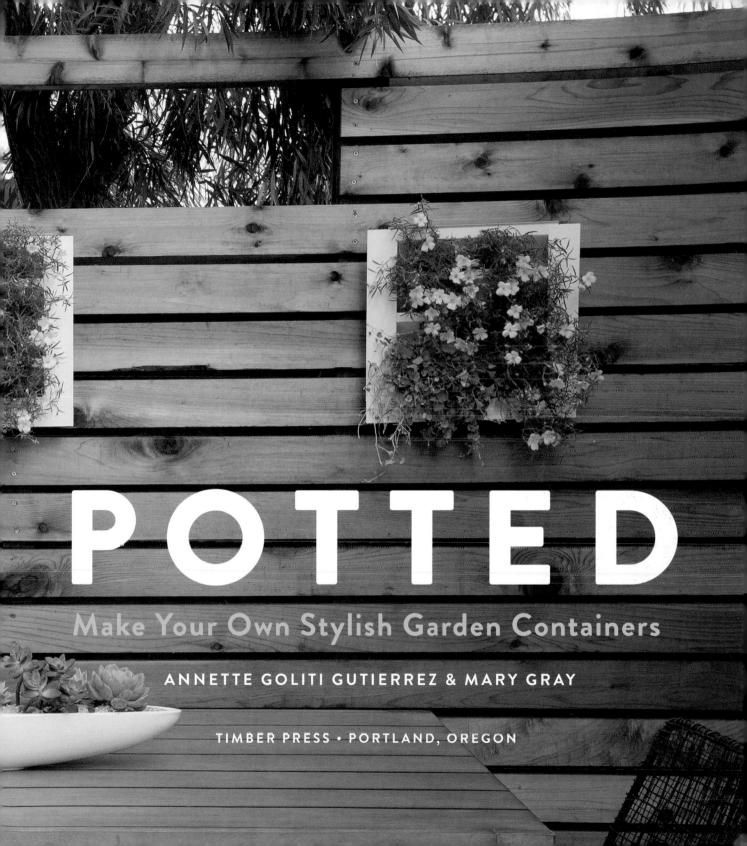

POTTED

Make Your Own Stylish Garden Containers

ANNETTE GOLITI GUTIERREZ & MARY GRAY

TIMBER PRESS • PORTLAND, OREGON

Photo credits appear on page 221.

The information in this book is true and complete to the best of our knowledge. All recommendations are made without guarantee on the part of the authors or Timber Press. The authors and publisher disclaim any liability in connection with the use of this information. Mention of trademark, proprietary product, or vendor does not constitute a guarantee or warranty of the product by the publisher or authors and does not imply its approval to the exclusion of other products or vendors.

Published in 2017 by Timber Press, Inc.
The Haseltine Building
133 S.W. Second Avenue, Suite 450
Portland, Oregon 97204-3527
timberpress.com

Printed in China
Text and cover design by Anne Kenady

Library of Congress Cataloging-in-Publication Data

Names: Gutierrez, Annette Goliti, author. | Gray, Mary, 1956- , author.
Title: Potted: make your own stylish garden containers / Annette Goliti
    Gutierrez and Mary Gray.
Description: Portland, Oregon: Timber Press, 2017. | Includes bibliographical
    references and index.
Identifiers: LCCN 2016036945 | ISBN 9781604696974 (pbk.)
Subjects: LCSH: Plant containers.
Classification: LCC SB418.4 .G88 2017 | DDC 635.9/86—dc23 LC record
    available at https://lccn.loc.gov/2016036945

A catalog record for this book is also available from the British Library.

A flying saucer planter made from industrial salad bowls and PVC piping.

To our wonderful Potted staff, who gave us the peace of mind and support we needed to work on this book wholeheartedly—but especially Sydney Michael, who held together our photography with her positive energy and endless hours of collaboration.

Common building materials are transformed into elegant planters by a poolside getaway.

CONTENTS

Our very first design was the Circle Pot, which was inspired by a 1960s hanging ashtray. Here it is planted with silver dollar plant (*Xerosicyos danguyi*) and ×*Graptoveria* 'Fred Ives'.

PREFACE

Whether you are a seasoned homeowner or are just starting out with your first garden patio, outdoor planters are seductive and sultry as they lure you in with their rich colors and clean lines. You can hardly wait to add them to your garden—until you see the price tag, which can be out of reach for many budgets. Big-box stores offer better bargains but fewer choices, and many of us are turned off by the idea of having the same thing as everyone else. We want unique products that make a statement. This book will help you boldly go where no planter has gone before by empowering you to create show-stopping containers.

We have owned Potted, a Los Angeles–based outdoor lifestyle brand, for more than a decade. As the creative forces behind the brand, we are always looking for unusual and interesting products geared toward outdoor living to excite and inspire our customers. It's one of the reasons we are a successful business and why many people choose us over the big chain stores. And while we support local artists and think nothing of traveling to find compelling products, what sets us apart are our Potted designs—garden pavers, tile tables, and especially pots (we are called Potted, after all).

So what does this mean for you? Well, our love of design compelled us to write this book, which is filled with inspirational and original ideas to help you make your own planters from everyday materials.

Beyond being affordable, we wanted to create projects that are gorgeous and accessible. You do not need a workshop or countless tools at your disposal to build these planters. We have a bit more expertise with fabrication than the average person, and this knowledge has been invaluable in working out how these projects assemble and whether they are feasible. When coming up with possible ideas, we asked ourselves three questions: is it affordable, are the materials easy to find, and could we do it on our own? If the answer to any of these questions was no, we threw out the idea. Finally, the most important consideration was that the finished product had to look fabulous.

We hope you will find ideas in this book that will excite and energize you to turn your own garden into a Potted oasis. There is something for everyone, from entryway planters crafted from garbage cans to hanging planters made with kitchenware. We have come up with designs we have never seen, and we offer a different spin on some familiar favorites. You can either follow our instructions exactly or, for even more fun, customize them to suit your own personality. And we expect Pinterest and Instagram to virtually explode with all your creations. We can't wait to see them. #pottedstylediy

DO IT YOURSELF BASICS

THINKING CREATIVELY ABOUT EVERYDAY MATERIALS

We conceived most of the ideas in this book while walking through building yards, home-improvement warehouses, and art-supply stores. By asking ourselves What if? as we perused the aisles, all sorts of possibilities came to mind. What if we put a back on that attic gable vent and hung it on the wall? What if we tried doing decoupage outdoors? What if we took a drywall mud pan and put some plants in it? If you allow yourself to see past an object's intended use, new worlds will open up to you.

The projects are organized by materials: concrete, plastic, metal, terra-cotta, and organic. You can do many projects with different materials than we specify. For example, the plastic garbage can could be metal; the terra-cotta planter could be wood. You could take concepts from one project and apply them to another—decoupage cinderblocks, anyone? Don't limit yourself to the materials we have presented. When you begin looking at everyday objects with a different eye, you will start to get crazy ideas. Try walking through your garage while wearing your anything-is-possible glasses. What could you do with an old lawn mower? We've limited our scope to new items you can purchase easily, but that doesn't mean you have to go shopping.

The original idea for this planter came from seeing a pile of cinderblocks in a building yard and wondering, What if?

TOOLS AND TIPS OF THE TRADE

We worked to come up with projects that do not require expensive or difficult-to-use tools. For the few times we couldn't avoid using things like circular saws, we suggest borrowing or renting them (unless you really catch the DIY bug, in which case get your own). And if you're afraid of particular tools, please ask for help. You do not have to do every last thing yourself. When we first started Potted, we were obsessed with tile and wanted to put it on everything (actually, we still do). We bought the least expensive tile saw known to humankind and began trying to figure it out. And even though we both learned to use it and made several tables, we were always a little scared, and we were relieved when we were doing well enough to hire someone to cut tile for us and could focus on design. You don't have to be the master of everything to do these projects.

You will want to use some tools over and over again, and developing a toolkit will come in handy. Here is a list of some must-have items.

ASSORTED DRILL BITS Some people don't realize there are bits to create holes and bits to screw things into objects. Unfortunately, both are referred to as drill bits. For our purposes, a set of assorted wood drill bits will cover most predrilling situations, and a standard two-sided Phillips head or straight head screw bit will cover the rest. Be sure you have a few masonry drill bits. These work for ceramics and concrete and are essential for drilling drainage holes. They get dull pretty quickly if you use them frequently, so be prepared to repurchase once in a while if you become addicted to DIY.

BOX CUTTER Also called a utility knife, this all-around tool works on more than boxes.

BUILDING ADHESIVES There are so many brands and different applications that it's important to read labels before you purchase. Look for whether the product is recommended for outdoor use, how long the setup time is (that is, how long you can work with it before it starts to harden), and what material it works best on (plastic, wood, concrete, fabric). Unless you are doing several projects at once, adhesives can be challenging to work with once they've been opened (another reason to buy the smaller, although more expensive, hand-squeezed tubes).

CAULKING GUN We use this constantly to apply building adhesives. However, you can buy most building adhesives in a hand-squeezed tube, so if you don't think you'll be doing a bunch of projects, you can skip this.

CLEANING KIT Adhesive remover, glass cleaner, canned air, clean rags, paper towels, and drop cloths will be very useful.

CORDLESS DRILL We use one in almost every project. No home should be without a cordless drill.

HAMMER In most of our projects we don't use a hammer for its usual purposes, but sometimes you just need to pound something.

HANDSAW AND MITER BOX For small jobs, a handsaw comes in handy, and a miter box will ensure your work is straight.

LEVEL A must for hanging things evenly.

MEASURING TAPE We like cloth and retracting tape versions.

PAINTER'S TAPE You'll use this for everything, including painting.

PAINTING KIT Keep an assortment of brushes, from very fine to 1 inch. Disposable foam brushes are good for edging or for brushing on glue. Stencil brushes work for stenciling (obviously). Plastic trays and rollers are also good to have on hand.

PLIERS Slip-joint pliers are the most common and are essential. Needle-nose pliers also come in handy in small spaces.

SAFETY KIT Goggles, gloves (leather and latex), and dust masks are the basic tools of the safety trade.

SANDPAPER You can use this to both smooth and rough up surfaces (that makes no sense, we know), and 100 grit sandpaper is a good all-around type. Higher grits are better for smoothing, and lower grits are more effective at roughing things up so adhesives and paint adhere better.

Anything can become a tool—even your husband's favorite strainer.

SCISSORS Everyone should have a pair of good sharp scissors.

WIRE CUTTERS We use these in several projects, and they are irreplaceable if you need to cut wire. Scissors are not intended for this purpose and will usually break, but nail cutters can work in a pinch.

DON'T GET HURT

This seems like an obvious statement, but it bears repeating. Don't get hurt. Common sense is the most important tool for any DIY project. If something seems unsafe, it probably is. We usually ask ourselves if we would let our kids use a particular tool. If the answer is no, we work with someone who has more experience. In addition, always work in a well-ventilated area when spraying or working with adhesives. Never use a power tool with a frayed or broken cord. Always protect your face and hands. And, finally, if you drink, don't drill. (We stole that from Matt Groening's "Life in Hell" cartoon, but it applies.)

A WORD ABOUT DRAINAGE

Every project in this book mentions drilling drainage holes. All plants (except water plants) want good drainage, or rot will eventually set in. Some plants, like succulents and cactus, will rot very quickly, so fast drainage is essential. Others, such as ferns or mosses, are more forgiving, but will eventually decay if they are never allowed to dry out. We understand that for some interior applications, especially centerpieces, it is not always possible to have drainage. For these situations we recommend using a layer of rock on the bottom to give the water a place to drain, but this is a temporary solution. You will need to replace these types of plantings every few months. But if you consider that freshly cut flowers survive about a week and your arrange-ment without drainage will last for roughly two months, it is a good investment (and you get the opportunity to make another arrangement when it needs replacing).

If drilling a hole in your planter just won't work, you can also turn your container into a cachepot. This word comes from the French verb *cacher* (to hide) plus pot—in other words, to hide a pot. In this case, you can leave your plant in its original nursery pot and allow the cachepot to hide it and essentially serve as a saucer. This method is far superior to planting in a container without drainage. Use Spanish, sheet, or sphagnum moss to hide the nursery container and give your planting a finished look.

The cinderblocks for this tiled planter were heavy and difficult to move, but worth the effort.

Sometimes drainage just isn't an option for a centerpiece. This container serves as a cachepot, with moss hiding the nursery pots, which contain golden club moss (*Selaginella kraussiana* 'Aurea') and satin pothos (*Scindapsus pictus* 'Argyraeus').

Concrete cinderblocks make
excellent planters, and the design
possibilities are endless.

CONCRETE

Concrete is made by combining Portland cement, water, and aggregate (rock or sand). You can manipulate it into many forms and applications. You can make your own concrete to create unique shapes with forms or molds, but many premade building supplies are also available.

Define a patio space with stylish rectangular planters.

THE MODERN RECTANGLE

Use backer board to create a hip contemporary planter.

———

Every week at Potted folks come in looking for lightweight concrete rectangle containers. These stylish, timeless pieces are used to solve many garden design issues. Two of the most popular applications are to create green privacy walls and define spaces. A visiting customer lamented that her small town in Oklahoma had no garden shops that carried anything like them. The larger rectangles were perfect for an open patio she wanted to make more private, but shipping was too expensive. This got us thinking, and we came up with backer board, a concrete product used for creating subfloors and tile backing. Backer board is easy to work with and readily available at home-improvement stores.

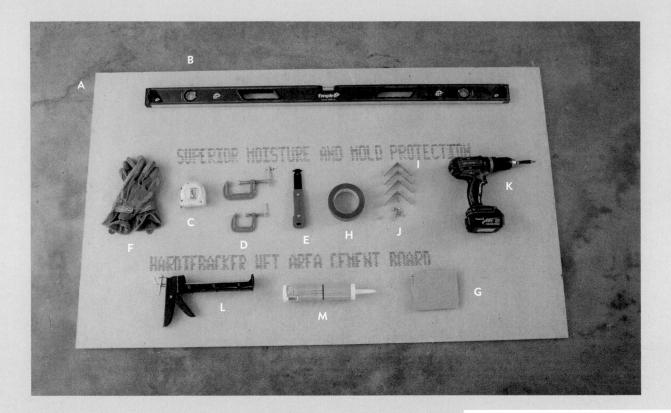

TOOLS & MATERIALS

A. One sheet 36 × 60 × ¼-in. backer board

B. 36-in. ruler or level

C. Measuring tape

D. Two C clamps

E. Scoring tool

F. Gloves

G. 100 grit sandpaper

H. Painter's tape

I. Twenty L brackets

J. ½-in. screws that fit L brackets

K. Drill with bit that fits ½-in. screws

L. Caulking gun

M. Waterproof caulk

Permanent marker (not pictured)

We wanted to delineate a separate patio for this pool house without cutting off the view of the pool. We chose an L shape to contain and create a cozy area while leaving one side open to invite you to the water.

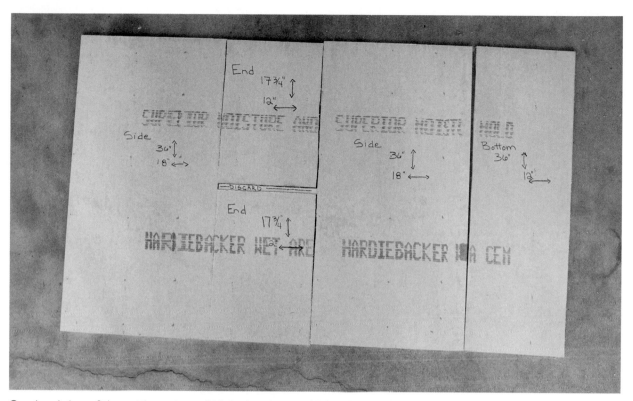

Overhead view of the cutting pattern (this is already cut, which makes it easier to see the pattern).

1 MEASURE AND CUT THE BACKER BOARD.

One piece of backer board will make one 36 × 12½ × 18-inch container. Use a measuring tape to mark off all the pieces you will need to cut. Remember, you have to allow for the thickness of the backer board to get the overall size correct, so you will need to adjust if you are making a different size.

We cut one 36 × 1-inch bottom, two 36 × 18-inch-long sides, and two 17¾ × 12-inch end pieces to make one planter. We placed our 36-inch-long sidepieces next to the 36-inch-long bottom piece. Then we placed our 12-inch end pieces on top of the bottom panel. Our bottom panel is ¼ inch thick, so we cut the height of the end pieces ¼ inch shorter so all the pieces were even on top. If you used ½-inch-thick backer board (also available), you would cut the end pieces ½ inch shorter.

Put the marked sheet of backer board on sawhorses or a table and use the C clamps to secure the level to the backer board. This gives you a hard line guide that stays in place while you score the board.

Scoring involves scratching an incision on the surface that creates a weakness and allows you to break the backer board cleanly without using a saw. It takes a little practice, so try it on some scrap pieces before you tackle the real thing. Wear gloves, as the constant pressure of bearing down on the scoring tool, along with its sharp edge, makes your hands susceptible to cuts and blisters. After you make your score mark, place the scored line just over the edge of the table and gently tap down. The piece should break off cleanly and easily. If it doesn't, try making your score marks deeper, and be sure to use sandpaper to smooth out any rough edges.

Tighten the clamps as much as possible to keep the level from moving.

Scoring allows you to cut the backer board without using a saw.

2 ASSEMBLE THE PIECES.

After you have cut all the pieces, put them together. Remember that the 12-inch end pieces go on top of the bottom panel, while the 36-inch-long side pieces sit flush with the bottom. Use the painter's tape to bind everything together until you screw in the brackets. An extra set of hands is helpful in this step.

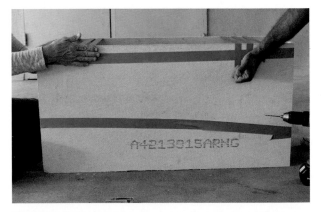

Bind the pieces together horizontally and across the top to hold them together.

Measure exactly where you will add your brackets.

3 MEASURE AND MARK BRACKET PLACEMENTS.

Using the measuring tape and marker, mark where you will install the L brackets. We placed them 1½ inches from the top and 1½ inches from the bottom. The middle one is in the center.

Using a bracket as your template, mark each bracket hole on all the sides.

4 SCREW IN HOLES AND BRACKETS.

Put it all together. Get one bracket on each corner first to give the planter strength as you screw in the other pieces. When you have screwed all the side brackets in place, turn the planter upside down to work on the bottom brackets. We placed one bracket on the center of each short panel and three brackets on the long panels. If your planter needs drainage, drill several holes in the bottom.

Predrilling your holes will make it easier to screw in the brackets.

TO PREDRILL MEANS to drill a hole the same size or smaller than the screw you are using, giving you a perfect guide for driving in your screw. You also can purchase an inexpensive adapter called a magnetic bit holder, which eliminates wobbling and slipping when driving in a screw. Either works, and both will help to give you a clean, professional look.

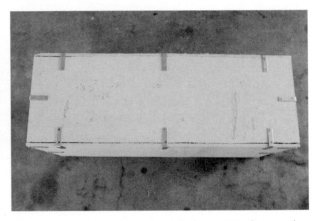

If you want your planter to have drainage, now is a good time to drill several holes in the bottom.

Starting at the bottom helps you avoid getting caulk on your clothing.

5 CAULK INSIDE SEAMS.

To avoid water and dirt seepage, seal the inside seams. Use the caulking gun to apply water-proof caulk around the bottom first. Then go from bottom to top on the four corners. Use a generous amount of caulk to ensure the seams are well covered. Follow the caulk manufacturer's instructions for dry time before proceeding. These contemporary planters are ready for their new home.

The finished planter with boxwood and vincas.

Candles glow inside this cinderblock planter.

CINDERBLOCK CANDLE WALL

Hot cinderblocks bring a spark to this DIY planter.

———

Years ago, we had a client who was an interior designer. We helped patioscape her midcentury home, and she had only one request: create something she had never seen before. This wasn't easy, but we found our spark of inspiration while scouting around a building-supply yard (one of our favorite things to do), where we came across a stack of cinderblocks. This was our eureka moment. Apartment Therapy featured our finished planter, and it was the beginning of a new DIY design trend.

To update this project, we decided to add a new element—fire. Now it is a mild-mannered planter by day and a party accessory by night. Turning some of the blocks on their sides and painting the interior provided the perfect illumination for flickering candles.

Original photo from our first cinderblock wall.

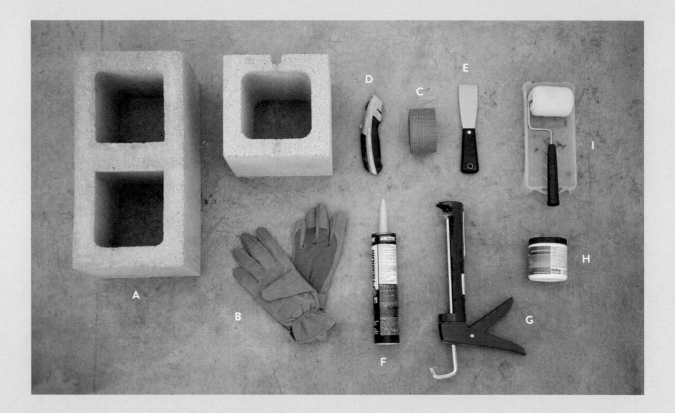

TOOLS & MATERIALS

A. Cinderblocks

B. Gloves

C. Cement board tape

D. Box cutter

E. Putty knife

F. Building adhesive

G. Caulking gun

H. Exterior paint

I. 4-in. paint roller and tray

Oliver agreed the wall would look perfect at the end of this patio.

PREPARING

First, decide where you want to create your planter. Once you build it, it's nearly impossible to move. Have the blocks delivered and set as close as possible to the site. Cinderblocks come in several different shapes, so there are countless variations on this theme. For this project we used the blocks most commonly employed when building walls. They measure 8 × 8 × 16 inches, so you must do a bit of calculating to determine how many to buy. You can also choose 8 × 8 × 8-inch single blocks, which will give you more options in your design. Sketch out something on paper so you have a template for calculating your materials.

WHEN CALCULATING MATERIALS, remember that an 8 × 8 × 16-inch block will really be ⅜ inch shorter to allow for mortar joints. If space is an issue, this might help.

Make sure you snap a photo of both sides of your wall so you know how to put it back together.

1 ASSEMBLE THE BLOCKS.

Put together the entire planter according to your sketches. Remember to use your legs when lifting, and go slowly. Wear gloves to protect your hands, as the blocks can be very rough. Move the blocks around until you are happy. Take several photos so you know how to put it back together.

When the design looks the way you want it, determine how many blocks will become planters so you can create screened bottoms that will keep the dirt inside. (However, if one planter block is sitting on the closed side of the block below, a screen isn't necessary.) Depending on the root growth of what you are planting, you may want to screen in open planters that are several blocks deep to minimize how much dirt you'll need.

2 SCREEN IN THE PLANTER BOTTOMS.

Gather the blocks that will become planters, and begin adding screens to the bottoms. (We used cement board tape, but heavy-duty plastic screen also works.) First, apply building adhesive along all the edges of the block to give the cement board tape extra strength (wet soil is heavy). Wear gloves when working with the adhesive, as it can be messy and difficult to get off your hands.

Crisscross the tape across the opening, placing it vertically and horizontally. Use the box cutter to cut off the tape at each end. Use the putty knife to push the tape into the adhesive so it gets a good grip. Follow the adhesive manufacturer's instructions for dry time before proceeding.

Lay a thick line of building adhesive all the way around the edges of the block.

Adhere several layers of tape to create a strong bottom.

Add extra adhesive to the top if you don't think the tape is coated well.

3 CONSTRUCT THE PLANTER.

Constructing the planter is the most time-consuming part of the project. Between every brick, use the caulking gun to apply a perimeter of building adhesive, then run a line across the middle to ensure the blocks stay secure. Wipe off any excess adhesive before it dries. Place the blocks carefully, following your photos.

Hide any grooves on your blocks against another block.

4 PAINT THE INSIDES.

For the blocks that will be candleholders, paint the insides to add dimension to your design. Follow the paint manufacturer's instructions for dry time before proceeding.

A small foam roller is perfect for getting inside the cinderblocks.

If you have extra bricks, try a few colors to see what works.

As it gets darker, the glass candleholders really start to glow in their painted blocks.

5 FILL THE PLANTER.

Double-check the cantilevered planters are dry before adding plants and candles. The growing space is small and the cinderblocks are porous and can dry out quickly, so drought-tolerant plants are a good choice. We decided to plant this wall as an herb garden, with a few succulents thrown in here and there. For candles, we used tealights in glass cups or bowls so we could see the flames. You are now ready to throw a garden dinner party, complete with freshly cut herbs and lovely candlelight ambience.

Prostrate rosemary will thrive almost anywhere, and it looks beautiful as it grows and begins to spill down.

A small amount of tile makes a big impression on these stacked cinderblocks.

TILED CINDERBLOCK PLANTER

Take a stacked cinderblock planter to another level.

___

As self-professed tile junkies, we will figure out a way to tile anything. In fact, that's how Potted began—we wanted garden pavers with inset tiles, but they didn't exist. We spent an entire summer figuring out how to perfect the technique, and when we were happy with our results, we set out to market them. But instead of selling the pavers to the first place we tried, we ended up buying the store instead—but that's another story.

Some of the first pavers we created at Potted, sited in a customer's garden.

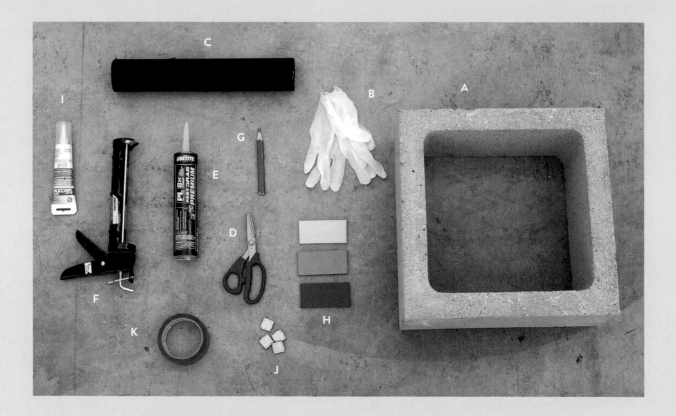

TOOLS & MATERIALS

A. Cinderblocks

B. Gloves

C. Nylon screen

D. Scissors

E. Waterproof building adhesive

F. Caulking gun

G. Pencil

H. Tile

I. Weatherproof silicone

J. Spacers

K. Painter's tape

Measuring tape (not pictured)

An example of Hillside Pottery. Today this piece is highly collectible and sells for thousands of dollars.

For this book, we wanted to create a tiled planter, but we worried that the same techniques we developed to create our pavers would prove too difficult to incorporate into a three-dimensional object. There is the crafting technique of gluing broken mosaic tile to a terra-cotta pot, but we wanted our version to have the more graphic feel of Hillside Pottery, a company from the early 20th century. After we saw a cute project our friend did with his daughters, where they glued tile onto a square cinderblock, we realized we could do the same thing. And it's so easy!

PREPARING

There are a couple of variables to ponder when preparing for this project: the size of the planter and the design of the tile. Concrete cinderblocks come in many shapes and sizes, but we found that square ones work best for this container. The 16 × 16 × 8-inch version is large enough to create a decent-size planter. The only variable is how high you want it to be. Consider aesthetics, as well as the size of the plant you want to use. We were designing the planter for a home with a large entryway, so we wanted to create a taller planter that would command some presence. We also took into account the other containers and plants with which we would be pairing it. This container is difficult to move, so make sure you are happy with its location.

There are endless possibilities for the tile design, which can be overwhelming. Start with what you already have, such as leftover tile from a kitchen or bathroom remodel. Take inspiration from your home's current decor. You may not want to make everything match, but something will spark an idea. For this project, the striking quality of the round pavers leading up to the front door influenced us. That, coupled with the strong red color of the building, encouraged us to be graphic and bold. You don't need much tile, so you can splurge on one special tile or get a bunch of samples from a local tile store and make a pattern. We used color tile samples from Heath Ceramics. Normally you have to buy a minimum of 25 square feet of each color, but we needed only one of each hue, so we purchased samples for a very low price. Once you have your tile, start playing with possible designs.

Potted-designed tile tables show examples of our designs.

1 SCREEN IN THE PLANTER BOTTOM.

The cinderblocks are open, so you will have to install a screen in the planter to keep dirt from falling out of the bottom. We wanted to create a taller planter, but we didn't need to fill the whole thing with soil, so we placed our screen between the middle and bottom blocks. If you are planting succulents or something else with very shallow roots, you could site your screen between the top and middle blocks. Conversely, if you are planting a larger plant, like a small tree, put the screen on the very bottom.

Cut the nylon screen into a square ¼ to ⅛ inch smaller than the cinderblock so it doesn't show on the sides when you place the next block on top. Set aside the screen. Use the caulking gun to squeeze a line of building adhesive around the top of the block. Wear gloves, as adhesive can can be difficult to get off your hands.

Lay your precut screen on the cinderblock. Use your gloved finger or a putty knife to push the screen into the adhesive. Apply another line of adhesive on top of the screen. This will give the screen more strength and help the two blocks stick together.

WHEN WORKING with a caulking gun, don't forget to use the attached metal prong to poke out the seal on your adhesive tube. Push the prong far into the tip and wiggle it around so it makes the biggest opening possible. This will make it easier to get the adhesive out.

Apply adhesive to all four sides with your caulking gun.

Nylon screen works better than metal, as it won't rust through

If you have a hard time getting the adhesive to come out, try using both hands to squeeze the caulking gun handle.

Resting the cinderblock on your thighs helps ease the weight and the stress on your back.

Apply a thick line of adhesive so it is strong enough to grab the bricks.

Make sure the blocks are perfectly aligned before adding the next one.

2 BUILD THE PLANTER.

Apply a thick line of building adhesive along the edge of the bottom cinderblock. Using your legs when lifting, place the next block on top. Make sure it is aligned perfectly. Wipe up any dripped or excess adhesive immediately, before it dries. Continue until your planter is the height you want.

Ready for tiling.

Don't assume a 4-inch tile is actually 4 inches—always measure. Handmade tiles often vary slightly, which can make a big difference when you're calculating spacing.

3 TILE THE BLOCK.

Lay out your tile design next to your finished planter. You will likely have to do a few calculations to ensure even spacing. To figure out our tile spacing from top to bottom, we measured the overall height and lay down our tiles using spacers to get the design as close as possible to those numbers on the top and the bottom. We needed to spread them out a little more, so we used small tiles as our spacers (instead of the plastic store-bought ones) because they were thicker and gave us more space.

We wanted to place the tiles exactly down the center of the planter. We measured the width of the tiles, subtracted that amount from the overall width of the cinderblock, and divided that amount in half to give us the starting point on the left side where we would lay the tiles. We used a measuring tape and pencil to mark the top and bottom of the block.

Using the two pencil marks as a reference, apply painter's tape to serve a guide for installing the tiles. You can also draw a straight line with your pencil and a ruler, but the tape is easier to see and remove.

Always measure both the top and the bottom of your planter to create a straight line guide.

Align the marks on the right side of the tape so you have a clean edge.

Apply enough silicone to give you good coverage, but not so much that it will squish out at the edges.

Push the lower tile against the spacers to ensure it is even.

And now the fun part: applying your design. Cut several 6-inch pieces of painter's tape and set them aside nearby. Although thinset (a tile adhesive) is the normal material used for adhering tile, weatherproof silicone is much easier for an application like this, and it works great. Squeeze a line of silicone around the back of the tile.

Place the tile firmly on the cinderblock, being very careful to align it perfectly with your tape guide. As soon as the tile is in place, put a piece of painter's tape over it to hold it until it fully dries. Apply silicone to the back of the next tile, and place it just underneath the first one, using the spacers to create an equidistant gap. Repeat this process until you have completed the design. Follow the silicone manufacturer's instructions for dry time before proceeding. Remove the tape, and voilà—your unique planter is ready to be planted.

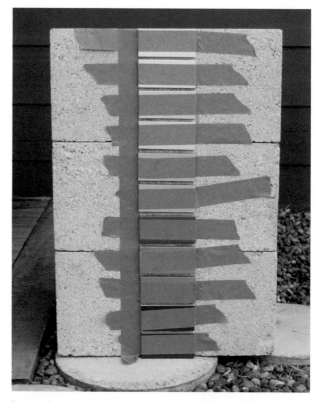

Leave the tape on for at least the minimum drying time on the silicone instructions.

This foxtail fern looks bold jutting out from the new planter.

Cut-up driveway grids make unusual planters on this patio.

TREADING THE WAY

Make a unique planter out of driveway grids.

———

With their graphic angles and modern repetition, driveway grids are just plain cool. Usually planted with lawn grass but sometimes filled with gravel, these grid systems make surfaces permeable, decreasing runoff to storm drains and beautifying your driveway. The grids are made of hard plastic or concrete, and there are several styles from which to choose. We found the diamond-shaped concrete versions most compelling.

These grids have an amazing geometric pattern, but their 2 × 3-foot size was a bit unyielding, so we decided to cut them up. They already come with a straight groove line that makes it easy to saw them precisely.

This driveway, laid with diamond-shaped grids and planted with grass, looks more like a patio than a place to park cars.

TOOLS & MATERIALS

A. Handheld skill saw with a concrete diamond blade

B. Driveway pavers

C. Safety goggles

D. Canned air

E. Spray paint

F. Heavy-duty nylon screen

G. Scissors

H. Latex gloves

I. Caulking gun

J. Waterproof building adhesive

Like all things made from concrete, this planter is heavy, and moving it around is difficult. Before you get started, decide where you want it and determine the best arrangement for your space. For this patio we wanted to create a statement around the modern bench, so we stacked the grids in a seemingly random pattern. However, there are limitless possibilities. We experimented with creating a low staggered-height fence. In another version we created a pony wall to hide an unsightly utility box. Where and how you use the grids will determine how many you will need to purchase. For each premade grid, you get three double diamonds that you can stack as desired.

1 CUT THE PAVERS.

Cutting the pavers is the most difficult part of the project, and there is no shame in asking someone else to do it for you. Saws can be scary and dangerous, but we were able to cut these pavers without chopping off our fingers—and we felt empowered in the process. Our advice is to go slow, wear safety goggles, and use a brand-new diamond blade, which is made to cut concrete.

These driveway grids are thicker than the average saw blade, so you will have to cut them from top and bottom to go all the way through. For the first cuts, use the prepoured drainage tracks as your guide to a get a straight line. Turn over the pavers. You will see the cut mark from your first pass. Put the blade right above it

Use the pre-existing lines on one side of the pavers as your guidelines for getting a straight cut.

and begin to cut again. This side should be easier, as it won't be as thick. If it suddenly seems too hard to move forward, you have probably moved off the cut line. Turn off your saw, reposition, and try again. Continue until you have cut as many pieces as you will need.

Our working photo of the design we wanted to execute.

2 TEST YOUR DESIGN.

Once you have cut all the pavers, it is time to play with the heaviest Legos you will ever use. Try different configurations. Experiment with height variations, and then stand back and assess your designs. Ask a friend for input, and take a photo of every composition so you remember all the possibilities. When you are happy with your creation, photograph it from a few angles. This will come in handy when you are putting it back together. If you are using more than one color, consider printing the photo and noting the color of each block. Total up how many of each color you will need, including those that will be on top.

3 PAINT THE PAVERS.

Your pavers must be clean before you prime them. If they are extremely dirty, scrub them with a stiff plastic brush. Let them dry completely before you paint them. If they look reasonably clean, canned air (used mainly for computers or photo equipment) works beautifully to blow off any hidden debris or dust.

Once the pavers are clean, you can spray-paint them. Prime the pavers first, or use a self-priming paint. From the list you made when you decided on your final design, gather the correct number of pavers and group them by color. Don't forget to separate or mark the pieces that will be painted on top. (If you were tiling, you would think of these as your bullnose or end tiles.) Follow the paint manufacturer's instructions for dry time before proceeding.

CANNED AIR also comes in handy when planting containers. Use it to blow off dirt that accidentally falls into flowers or leaves, which can ruin a specimen display.

Use canned air to blow dirt and dust off your pavers.

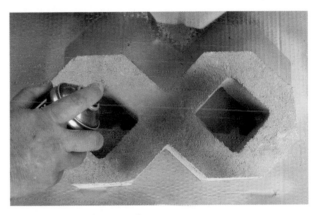

Spray-painting the top of a paver.

Drying pavers.

When cutting out your screen, be sure you make it large enough that the adhesive has something to hold on to.

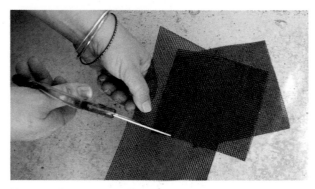

Use your first screen as a pattern for cutting out the rest.

Apply adhesive to the paver.

4 SCREEN IN THE PLANTER BOTTOM.

The pavers are open, so you will have to install a screen in the planter to keep dirt from falling out of the bottom. Heavy-duty nylon screen works well for this project. We had planned to plant our container with moss, which has very shallow roots, so we made only the top paver the planter. If your plant has deeper roots, screen in the bottom paver.

Hold a corner of screen over one paver opening and eyeball the size as you cut it out with scissors. You can also use a measuring tape, but that can be difficult for something this small. Once you have made your first screen, use it as a pattern to cut out the rest. You may have to blunt a few corners by cutting the tips diagonally so they don't stick out on the side.

Put on latex gloves. Use the caulking gun to squeeze out a thick layer of adhesive on the unpainted bottom of the paver. Press one screen firmly into the adhesive, making sure it really takes hold. Follow the adhesive manufacturer's instructions for dry time before proceeding.

Attach the screen with your gloved hands.

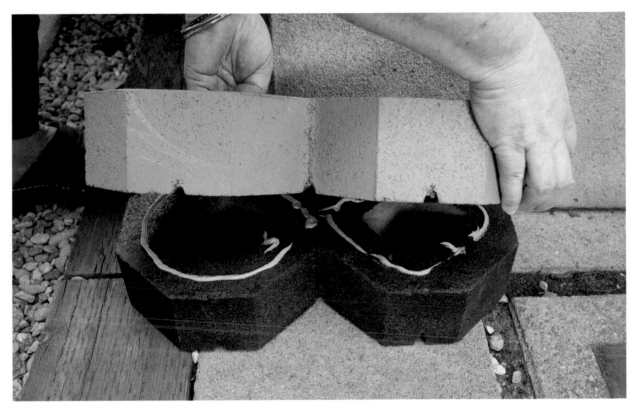

Putting the final pieces together.

5 BUILD THE PLANTER.

Apply a thick line of building adhesive along the edge of the bottom paver. Place the next paver on top, and make sure it is aligned perfectly. Refer to your photo to make sure you are following your vision. If you make a mistake, don't panic: you have 15 to 20 minutes before the adhesive becomes too difficult to pull apart. If you do have to correct an error, be sure to add additional adhesive.

You are now ready to plant. For a container with small openings, ground covers, sedums, and succulents are excellent choices. We used Scotch moss in dark green and chartreuse because it looked cute tufting out of the top of the new planters, and anything tall would have overpowered the bench. You could also try very narrow, tall plants like sansevieria or certain varieties of senecio. If you do this, make your planters deeper by putting the screened bottom at least two pavers down to allow for enough root growth. No matter what plants you decide to use, they will love their new home in this very unusual planter design.

Succulents spill out of a cement tile planter.

CEMENT TILE CUSTOM CONTAINER

Fashion a durable container that is perfect for hard outdoor use.

Like many people in the design world, we are totally in love with cement tile. It is graphic, colorful, and so beautiful. Often mistakenly referred to as encaustic tile, cement tile has long been used throughout Europe and South America as striking, durable flooring. These bright patterns have also started to creep into modern bathroom and kitchen backsplashes. The tiles are produced in South America, Mexico, and Morocco, but they are available in tile stores throughout the world.

At Potted we use cement tile to make outdoor tables. They are unusual, eye-catching, and extremely heavy (no chance of blowing away in the wind). One day we realized that our leftover tiles would make interesting garden planters, and we were on another DIY adventure.

A stunning kitchen by Design Vidal in Los Angeles centers around the company's own cement tile.

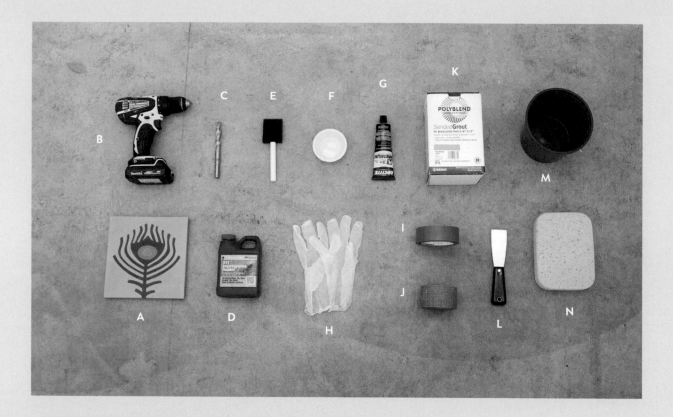

TOOLS & MATERIALS

A. Five 8-in. cement tiles

B. Drill

C. ½-in. masonry drill bit

D. Sealer

E. Foam brush

F. Container to hold sealer

G. Waterproof building adhesive

H. Latex gloves

I. Painter's tape

J. Cement board tape

K. Sanded grout

L. Putty knife

M. Mixing bucket

N. Tile sponge

PREPARING

Choose four tiles to create the outside of the container, but you don't have to limit yourself to four identical ones. We chose a peacock feather pattern from Design Vidal that covers two tiles, and wrapped it around the side to create the complete image. You could also choose four completely different tiles, or use four of the same and place two vertically and two horizontally. Cement tile offers so many possibilities and different patterns that you will have no shortage of ideas.

1 SEAL THE TILE.

Cement tile is extremely porous. You must seal it, or it will stain—especially during grouting. Begin by thoroughly cleaning your tile with a damp rag to remove all dust and debris. Allow the tile to dry completely before you apply sealer. Use a penetrating sealer and a foam brush, and work in a well-ventilated area. Apply two coats to seal. Most sealers dry to the touch in 10 minutes. They don't become completely active for up to 24 hours, but you will need to wait for your adhesive to fully dry before grouting, so the timing works out perfectly. You do not have to seal the bottom tile.

Apply at least two coats of sealer to clean tiles.

Drill a drainage hole in the bottom tile.

Hold the base tile while applying the adhesive.

2 CREATE A DRAINAGE HOLE.

Make a drainage hole in the bottom tile before you put the planter together so you don't put too much stress on the grout joints. Drill a ½-inch hole with the masonry drill bit. (You can drill several smaller holes if you have a smaller bit.) If you're planning to use the planter as a cachepot, skip this step.

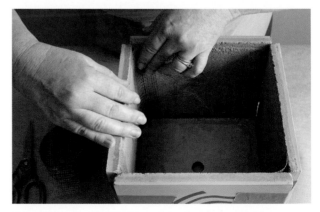

Use painter's tape to hold the tiles together while they dry.

3 ASSEMBLE THE PLANTER.

Put on latex gloves. Squeeze out a thick line of building adhesive on all four sides of your base tile. (The tube version of adhesive is easy to work with.) Adhere your four main tiles to the base tile. Use painter's tape to steady each corner until all sides are in place. Follow the adhesive manufacturer's instructions for dry time before proceeding.

Push the cement board tape into the corners with your fingers.

Using your finger is the easiest way to apply the adhesive to bond the tape.

Cut the cement board tape into four pieces that will fit along the length of each inside corner of your planter. This tape is self-adhesive, so it should stay in place when you push it into the edge. If the tape does not stick, try turning it over.

Use your gloved finger (it's hard to get the tube inside the container) to apply more building adhesive over the cement board tape to strengthen the bond. Follow the adhesive manufacturer's instructions for dry time before proceeding.

Make sure to cover all the tape with adhesive to create a strong bond.

CEMENT BOARD TAPE also makes a fantastic screen for covering drainage holes so dirt doesn't fall out of the bottom.

4 GROUT THE PLANTER.

Normally you would use nonsanded grout for cement tiles, which are designed to fit together very closely when laid as a floor. But your grout joint in this planter will be very large, so it is important to use sanded grout for better strength (nonsanded will crumble very easily). We chose gray because the middle of the peacock feather is the same color, and we wanted to make it stand out.

Pour about 1 inch of dry grout into your mixing bucket. You won't need very much, as you are grouting only four corners. Slowly pour in water and mix until the grout is the consistency of cookie dough. Wait 5 minutes, and then mix again.

Use the putty knife to push the grout into each corner, pressing enough in the center that you fill the entire crevice. Scrape the knife from bottom to top to remove excess, and smooth out the grout with a wet tile sponge. (You can cut the sponge to a smaller size to make it easier to work with.) Move the sponge lightly up the grout line. Do not press too hard, or you will create gouges in your grout. Clean extra grout off the tile as you go, as dried grout is nearly impossible to remove later. Let everything dry for 10 to 15 minutes. Lightly wipe the tiles one more time to remove any grout haze that may have developed. Make sure the sponge is well rinsed (or use a fresh one) so you don't add haze instead of taking it off. Follow the grout manufacturer's instructions for dry time before proceeding.

The grout should look like cookie dough when it's ready.

Push grout into the corner opening.

Scrape the knife from bottom to top to remove any excess grout.

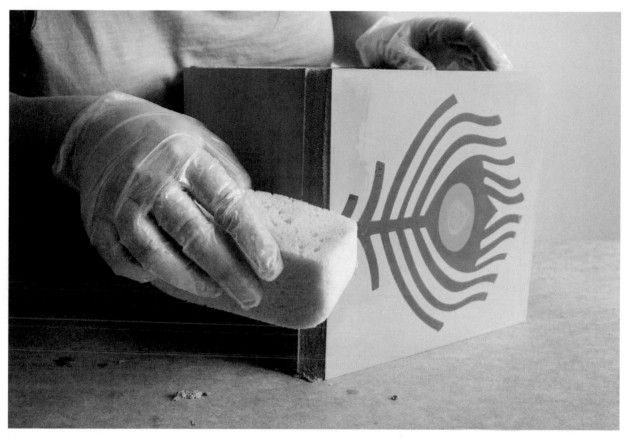

Use a wet sponge to smooth out your grout.

5 SEAL THE GROUT.

After the grout has completely dried, use the foam brush and penetrating sealer to seal the grout. You can also seal the tiles again, if you have the time and inclination. Your new container is now ready to plant and enjoy.

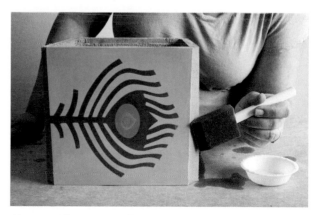

Always seal your grout lines to avoid stains later.

A plastic vent cover
transformed into a
wall planter.

PLASTICS

People often turn up their noses at the mention of a plastic planter, but plastic offers so many options that it's shortsighted to dismiss it. Affordable, accessible, and easy to work with, PVC pipe alone has so many possibilities we could create an entire project book using only that material. Maybe next time.

A cascading arrangement of violas, lamb's ear, and sweet mint welcomes visitors at the front door.

TOTALLY TUBULAR PVC PLANTER

A compact cluster of PVC tubes makes a fetching bouquet.

———

Plants are a reminder of the ever-changing beauty of nature, and they can lift your mood instantly. How lovely to make the walkway to the front door more welcoming with a striking composition of greenery in an unexpected arrangement. For this project, we created a statement piece out of PVC tubes we saw while scouting the aisles of our local home-improvement store. Alone the 4-inch pipe didn't seem significant, but when we imagined it as a bouquet, we saw so many possibilities.

Because PVC is such a recognizable material, we wanted to find a clever way to disguise it. Initially we were going to sand all the tubes and spray-paint them, but a happy accident changed our minds. Sanding revealed a matte charcoal patina, and it was so pretty we decided to go with it. We then opted for a stenciled design for embellishment. We chose this design for the graphic circular pattern that reinforced the shape of the tubes and overall design of the planter.

TOOLS & MATERIALS

A. 4-in. dia. PVC plumbing pipe

B. 4-in. all-ABS snap-in drain for each tube

C. Backsaw or electric jigsaw

D. Painter's tape

E. 180 fine grit sandpaper

F. Permanent marker

G. Stencil

H. Acrylic clear gloss outdoor spray paint

I. Drill with Phillips head

J. 1-in. screws with Phillips head

Measuring tape (not pictured)

Before you begin, you need to decide how big your bouquet will be so you know how many 10-foot tubes to purchase. Get a little extra to allow some room to play; what you initially pictured might look different when you put it together.

READY-MADE stencils are readily available. Home-improvement stores will carry an adequate inventory, but art-supply shops have the best selection. There are also on-line sites or DIY blogs that offer downloads for a small fee or sometimes even free.

Mark your cut lines.

Wrap the painter's tape evenly just below your mark.

1 MEASURE, MARK, AND CUT THE PVC TUBE.

Using a measuring tape and marker, note where you want to make cuts on the tubes. We cut our eight tubes into 5-, 7-, 9-, 12-, 15-, 20-, 23-, and 28-inch lengths. Use painter's tape at the cutting line to keep from angling the saw while you cut. Turn the tube as you saw. When you have gone all the way around, the tubes should separate easily.

Turn the tube as you saw to make sure you keep the cut straight.

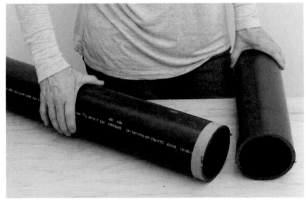

When you have gone all the way around, the tubes should come apart cleanly.

Long strokes will give you even, clean sanding marks.

2 SAND THE TUBES AND CONFIGURE THE ARRANGEMENT.

Sand lightly up and down each tube in long, even strokes. Avoid deep scratches and stay in straight vertical lines; you want to take the gloss and writing off the PVC and leave it with a matte charcoal finish. Don't forget to sand the end of the tube that will be the top.

After sanding, play with the arrangement, as your initial idea may look better with a different configuration. Consider adding or taking away one or two tubes. Take pictures as you work so you can recall what you like best.

Snap a photo of the final arrangement to help you remember how to put it back together.

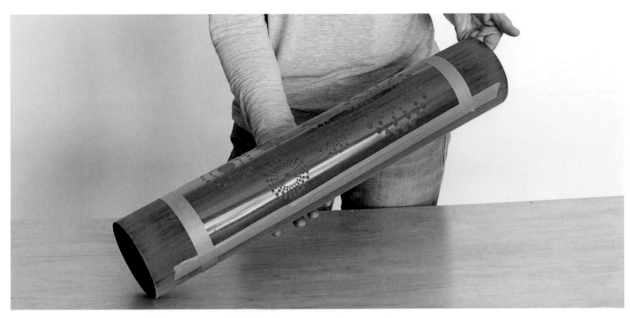

Make sure the stencil is lying as flat as possible so the images come out crisp.

3 APPLY AND SPRAY-PAINT THE STENCIL DESIGN.

When stenciling, start with the longer tubes, as this is where most of the pattern will be. Lay the stencil pattern on the tube, and tape it down along the sides and top (keep in mind that parts of it won't be visible when all the pieces are screwed together). Make sure it is snug where the cutouts are so you get a crisp line with the spray paint. To avoid overspray, tape far enough along the outside or use newspaper or plastic to cover the portion of the tube that isn't being stenciled. On shorter tubes, cut the stencil as needed to fit.

Spray in a well-ventilated area and use a mask if you work indoors. Spray-paint two light coats, which will reduce dripping, and allow the first coat to dry before applying the second. Follow the paint manufacturer's instructions for dry time before proceeding.

Avoid holding the can too close to your tube when you spray, or you will get drips.

The drain discs have wide openings. If you are concerned about dirt falling out, you can add a plastic screen to the inside.

4 ATTACH THE SNAP-IN DRAIN DISC.

Put in the snap-in drain so your planters will have good drainage. These discs are made for PVC pipe, so this is easy to do.

Hold the pieces firmly. It will take some force to get the screw through both pipes.

The planter all screwed together.

5 ATTACH THE TUBES TOGETHER.

After you have installed all the drains, separate out the two shortest pieces to begin attaching them to each other. Refer to your photo to make sure you are attaching the correct pieces. With your drill, screw at an angle down about 2 inches from the rim of the shortest tube into the other tube. If you have trouble getting the screws in, try predrilling the holes before screwing. Attach the pairs together, screwing the shorter one to the longer tube until all the tubes are secured.

Attached the two tallest tubes together, then the next two in descending order of height. Ultimately you will have four pair of tubes. Next, screw the four sets together, again starting with tallest and working your way to shortest, until the planter is a single unit. Your bouquet planter is ready for its new life filled with the plants that make you smile.

4169

Painted tubes of PVC make a strong statement in this entryway, beautifully enhancing the ponytail palm and furcraea.

THAT'S A
WRAP

PVC tubes create an attractive wraparound pot cover.

——————

We can't stop thinking about PVC. Inexpensive, colorful, readily available, and easy to work with, it has everything we are looking for, but we wanted to find a way to use it for building a larger container. Although PVC tubes are available by special order in larger sizes, they start getting quite expensive, defeating the whole purpose of DIY. While looking at bamboo fencing, we were inspired to string together smaller PVC pipes with wire to create a decorative wrap for a nursery container. The beauty of this technique is that you can make the cover any size you want.

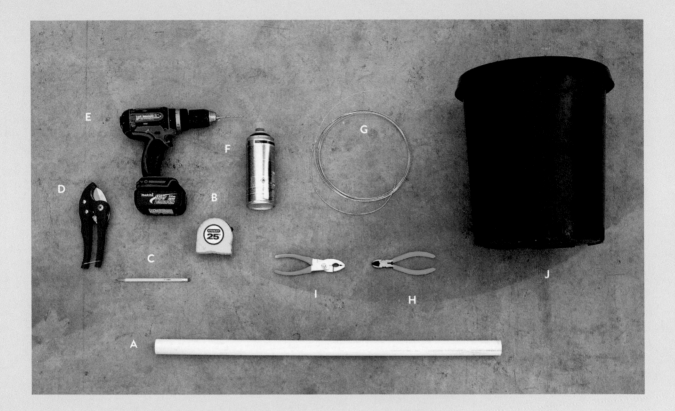

TOOLS & MATERIALS

A. 1¼-in. outside dia. PVC tube

B. Measuring tape

C. Pencil

D. PVC pipe cutter

E. Drill with ⅛-in. bit

F. Self-priming spray paint

G. Wire

H. Wire cutter

I. Pliers

J. 5-gal. nursery container

Size is the main thing to consider for this project. You can cut the pipe to any height you want, so there is no limit to how large the planter can be. You can even adjust the diameter to accommodate a saucer and hide any trays. We used 1¼-inch pipe for this project, but PVC is available in any home-improvement store in ½- to 4-inch sizes, so you have a lot of choices.

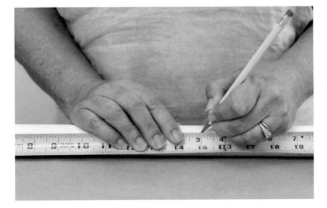

Measure and mark the pipe where you need to cut.

The PVC cutter has a ratchet lever that makes it very easy to cut the pipe.

1 MEASURE AND CUT THE TUBES.

First, calculate your materials. The height of the planter was easy to determine: the nursery pot was 14 inches tall, so we wanted our pipe length to be 15 inches to give us a little camouflage. From a standard-length 10-foot pipe we knew we could get eight 15-inch pieces. To figure out how many 10-foot pipes we needed to purchase, we divided the circumference of the widest area of our planter (if you are going to cover a saucer, use the circumference of its outer edge) by the diameter of the pipe. Our nursery pot was 43 inches in circumference, including the rim. Divided by 1.25 we got 34.4. We rounded up to 35 pieces of 15-inch lengths. We divided 35 by 8 (the number of 15-inch lengths in a 10-foot pipe) and got 4.375. Rounded up, we needed to buy five 10-foot pipes.

The PVC cutter is a handy tool that is much easier to use than a hacksaw for smaller pipes. Make sure you buy one that works for the diameter pipe you need to cut. Keep your cuts straight so you don't get uneven edges, and measure precisely.

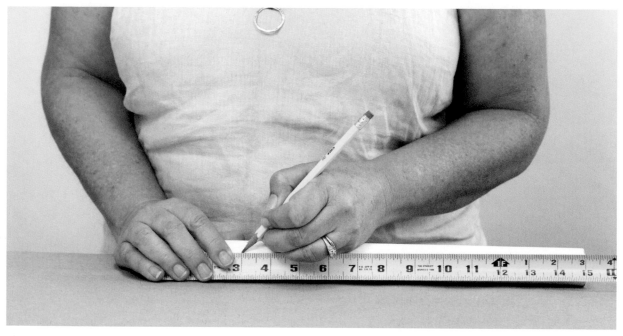

Measure your drill holes precisely.

2 MEASURE AND DRILL WIRE HOLES.

Measure and drill wire holes before you paint your pipes so you don't ruin your paint job with too much handling. We marked 3 inches from both ends. The PVC pipe is rigid and unlikely to flop around, so two strands of wire is sufficient for most sizes. Again, be precise in your measuring: if your holes are off, the pipes will be uneven. The old saying "Measure twice, cut once" is good to remember here.

Drill the holes for the wire very carefully: if the holes are uneven, the pipes will be too. Put the pipe on the edge of a table or workbench, hold it securely, and drill straight down.

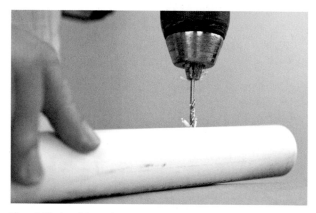

The drill should go through the soft plastic easily.

To finish the tubes, make sure to spray the inside of at least the top of each one.

3 SPRAY-PAINT THE PIPES.

Before you paint, use pencil to mark the color of each tube. Establish your pattern, taking care to think about how it will terminate; the goal is to repeat the design all the way around. We used three black, one blue, one green.

Spray-painting takes more time than you might think. Each tube has a lot of surface area to cover, and there are 35 tubes in this project. We used self-priming spray paint to eliminate one step, but you can prime if you wish. We found that loosely hanging the pipes on the wire helped ensure each length was sufficiently covered and allowed to dry before the next step.

4 WIRE THE PIPES TOGETHER.

Use your wire cutter to cut two lengths of wire that are 10–12 inches longer than the total circumference of the desired diameter (so you have room at the end for tying it off). Lay down your pipes in the correct order of color, and begin threading them onto the wire like beads on a string. We put a 3- to 4-inch bend at the beginning of both wires so the first pipes wouldn't fall off as we added more, and also to allow for extra wire to tie them together when we were finished. Continue until all the pipes are snugly threaded on the wire and you have a few inches of extra wire on both ends.

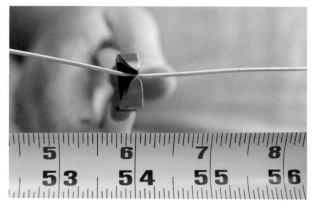

Make sure to cut your wire at least 10 or 12 inches longer than the total circumference.

5 FASTEN THE ENDS TOGETHER.

Once you have placed all the tubes onto the wire in the correct order, put the whole piece around your nursery container, and twist together the two end wires as tightly as possible. Do a couple of twists by hand to get it started, and then use the pliers to twist as far as you can without breaking the wire. After you have finished, use the wire cutters to trim the ends as closely as possible, then push the twist between the two pipes. And that, as they say in the film industry, is a wrap.

Thread each pipe onto the wire in the correct color order.

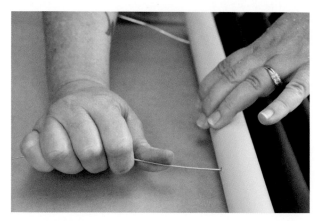

Firmly pull each new tube against the last one so they are nice and snug.

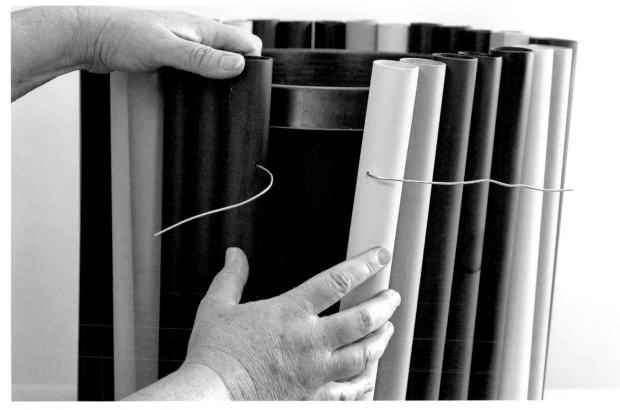

Pull the planter together to finish.

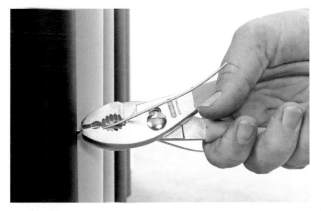

Pliers will help you tighten the wire.

Use wire cutters to clean up the ends.

From roofing vent to vertical garden.

ROOF
VENT WALL
POUCH

This industrial-chic wall planter will attract hordes of admirers.

———

On our continuing quest to build amazing vertical gardens in tight spaces, we literally stumbled upon these roof pipe vent covers at our local building-supply store after someone left a pile on the floor. Lying at our feet like an offering from the DIY gods, they needed only a couple of minor modifications to become a wonderful wall planter.

These practical pockets can add lush life wherever you are short on space. We found the perfect place for these versatile little pouches at an industrial-modern-meets-cottage home, where the patio was calling out for a bit of green to soften the sparse environment.

TOOLS & MATERIALS

A. Roof pipe vent

B. Permanent marker

C. Scissors

D. Box cutter

E. Drill with ⅛-in. drill bit

F. Medium to coarse grit sandpaper

G. Metal flashing panel

H. Caulking gun

I. Waterproof adhesive

J. Level

K. 1-in. screws

L. ½-in. washers

M. 1-in. plastic anchors (for stucco walls only)

When designing, making informed choices is half the battle. From the beginning, we committed to minimal decor and minimal care. Translation: Don't go nuts and cover the whole wall. We chose to do an up-and-down pattern to reflect the angle of the corrugated metal wall and the upward movement of the steps. We then selected plants that would stay small and were easy to care for.

Mark the vent pouch where you want to cut it.

Scissors work well to cut the soft rubber.

When using a box cutter, always cut away from yourself in case your hand slips.

1 CREATE THE POUCH.

The front panel of the roof vent is soft rubber with a hole in the middle for a pipe. To modify it and create a planting pocket, we cut off the top half, leaving the bottom intact to create a pouch. With the marker, indicate where you want to cut. Use scissors to cut across the width of the rubber in both directions from the center hole. With the box cutter, cut out the rubber in the ridge where it meets the hard plastic of the shell. Be sure you're cutting off the shallower side of the vent, leaving the deeper side, which will hold more dirt, to be used as the bottom of the planter.

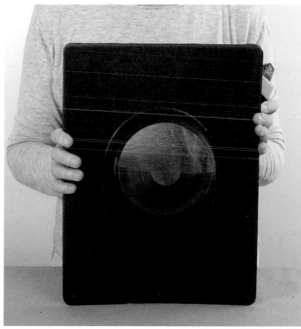
Roof vent with the top cut off.

2 CREATE DRAINAGE HOLES.

If you want drainage, mark holes on the bottom of the pouch, then drill them out. If you don't need drainage, skip this step.

Mark the drainage holes.

Drill the drainage holes.

3 GIVE THE PLANTER A BACK.

It is important to create a back for the planter so water and dirt do not seep out of the back and mar the wall. Before you can attach the metal flashing panel to the roof vent, you need to prepare both surfaces so the smooth metal and the smooth plastic can create a bond. Use the sandpaper to rough up the back area of the vent and the front of the metal flashing panel where the two will attach.

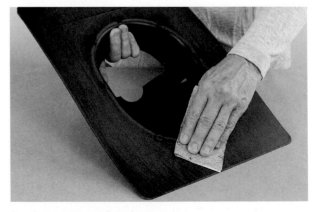

Sandpaper the roof vent.

With the back of the pocket facing up, center the metal flashing panel and mark the corners so you know how it fits onto the back. Remove the panel. Use the caulking gun to squeeze out a thick line of adhesive all the way around the opening.

Place the metal flashing panel on the pouch, lining it up with the marks. Press down firmly all the way around to create a good bond. If any adhesive oozes out of the sides, wipe it away immediately before it dries.

Turn over the completed wall pouch so the back is against the table. Again, press firmly all the way around. You can put books or other heavy objects on the corners while the adhesive dries to ensure a really good hold. Follow the adhesive manufacturer's instructions for dry time before proceeding.

Sandpaper the metal flashing panel.

Apply the adhesive generously.

Press firmly when attaching the metal back.

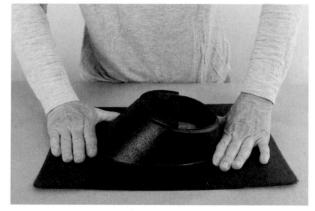
Applying pressure will help create a strong bond.

A level will help you hang the pouches straight.

Play with placement before you attach the pouches to the wall.

4 INSTALL THE POUCHES.

Each installation is site specific, but there are standard guidelines to follow. First, decide how you are going to arrange the pouches. Once you have determined placement, find the middle of the space. There are four for this installation, so we marked the middle and then the middle of each half, which created four compartments (one for each pouch).

Use the level to make sure each pouch is straight and that the alternating design is in line and evenly spaced. Use the washers with the screws to provide support and prevent the plastic from tearing. Use the plastic wall anchors for stucco walls if that's where you are hanging them. When your friends come over and admire your new wall planters, enjoy their looks of astonishment when you tell them the chic planters were once roof pipe vents.

Screw each corner onto the wall for strength.

Finished pouches planted with trailing foliage.

Divide a space beautifully with
a green privacy screen.

DIVIDE AND PLANT

Is it a door or a green privacy screen? It's both!

With more people growing their own food and urban dwellers looking for new ways to incorporate plants into their living spaces, it is easy to see why vertical planting has exploded in the gardening world. It maximizes space and can create instant privacy while delineating different living areas.

We wanted our vertical garden to address issues of privacy and mobility. For daily use and small gatherings, creating a wall between the seating area of this patio and the outdoor shower was a great way to separate the two spaces and keep it green. However, we also wanted this screen to be portable and easily moved out of the way for larger parties.

TOOLS & MATERIALS

A. Wood door (not hollow)

B. Drop cloth

C. Measuring tape

D. Handsaw

E. Miter box

F. Angle square

G. Two 1 × 6 × 36-in. redwood fence planks

H. Four pieces 1 × 2 × 16-in. redwood molding

I. Four pieces 1 × 3 × 22-in. redwood molding

J. Hacksaw

K. Drill

L. Phillips head driver bit

M. ⅛-in. drill bit

N. 1½-in. wood screws

O. Dust mask

P. Safety goggles

Q. 100 grit sandpaper

R. Painter's tape

S. Paint tray, roller, brushes

T. Pad sander

U. Canned air

V. 1 qt. per color of outdoor flat latex paint

W. Six pieces 24-in.-long PVC rain gutter

X. Twelve matching gutter brackets

Y. Twelve matching gutter end caps

PREPARING

This door planter fills all sorts of needs, from blocking out an annoying neighbor to beautifying a window view in an awkward area. Once you determine its use, you can decide how to customize it. Will it be two-sided like ours, so it's lovely on both sides? Should it be freestanding or can it hang from the top?

You can purchase a new wood door at any lumberyard or home-improvement store. Avoid hollow doors, which are usually used for interior closets. They are inexpensive but made from laminate, which will come apart quickly outdoors. For less pricey alternatives, try your local Habitat for Humanity store, salvage yards, or even tag sales. You may even have an old door taking up space in the garage.

1 CUT WOOD FOR THE DOOR BASE.

You will need to create a sturdy base so the door can stand safely without being hung. Using the miter box and handsaw, cut the molding pieces to size. Cut the 1 × 3 × 2-inch pieces at a 45-degree angle on both sides to brace the bottom plank to the door (the guide on your miter box will give you the correct angle). Cut the 1 × 2 × 16-inch pieces straight across. Wear safety goggles while sawing.

Angle cut with the miter box and saw.

2 PREPARE AND PAINT THE DOOR AND FRAME PIECES

The condition of the door will dictate the amount of prep needed before painting. The door should be as smooth and free of old paint as possible. If it needs heavy sanding, use the pad sander, which will cover a larger area much more easily than sanding by hand. If the door is in fairly good condition, a quick hand sand will be sufficient. Sand the pieces for the frame too. Wear a dust mask while sanding.

When you have finished sanding, wipe down all the pieces to remove small fragments of dust and debris. Our door also had louvered vents, so we used canned air to blow out dust in hard-to-reach places. Protect your work area with a drop cloth. Paint the door and all individual support pieces before attaching them together. For a two-color combination, tape off the accent area and paint the door with the roller. Remove the tape and paint in the accent color with a foam brush to ensure a clean line. Follow the paint manufacturer's instructions for dry time before proceeding.

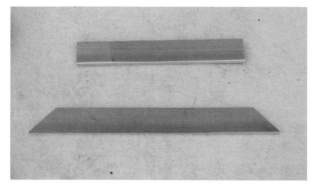

Examples of 45-degree angle and straight cuts.

Painted wood pieces needed for the door supports.

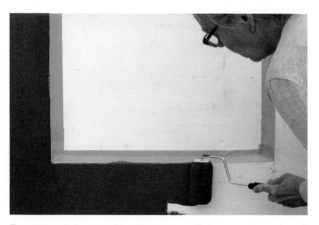

For a two-color combination, tape off the accent area and paint the door with the roller.

Remove the tape and paint in the accent color. Use the foam brush to get a clean line.

3 ATTACH THE DOOR BASES.

Have someone hold the door while you attach the bottom. Rest the door on its side. Doing one side at a time, place the 1 × 6 × 36-inch redwood fence plank flush with the edge of the door, and center it evenly so you have the same distance on either side. Use the drill to screw in three screws to attach the base. If you have a hard time getting the screws to go in, predrill the holes. Do the same thing on the other side.

Three screws give the bottom more strength.

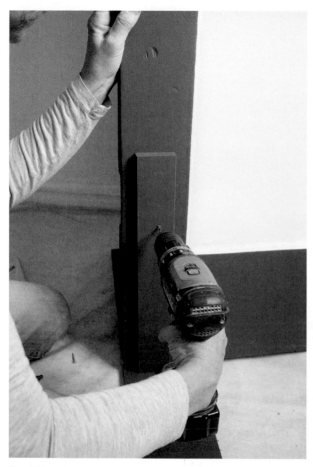

Predrill and screw the vertical wood piece in place.

Predrill and screw the angled wood piece to the side of the wood support section on the door.

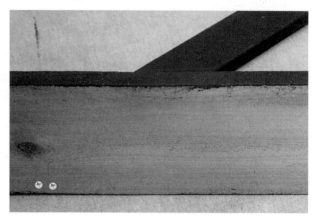

Screw the base plank into the angled wood from the underside with two screws.

Next, create the braces for the base. Place the 1 × 2 × 16-inch flat-cut section of wood vertically up against the door 1 inch in from the edge, and rest it directly on the base. Predrill and screw into place at the top and the bottom. Do this on all four sides.

Finally, position the angle-cut 1 × 3 × 22-inch wood pieces so the angles are flat against the base plank and the door. Use the angle square to help you keep all the pieces at the correct angles. Predrill and screw the top piece into place with two screws. Repeat this process for the three remaining supports. After all four are attached at the top, set the door on its side so you can screw in the angled wood that is resting on the plank base from the bottom on all four supports.

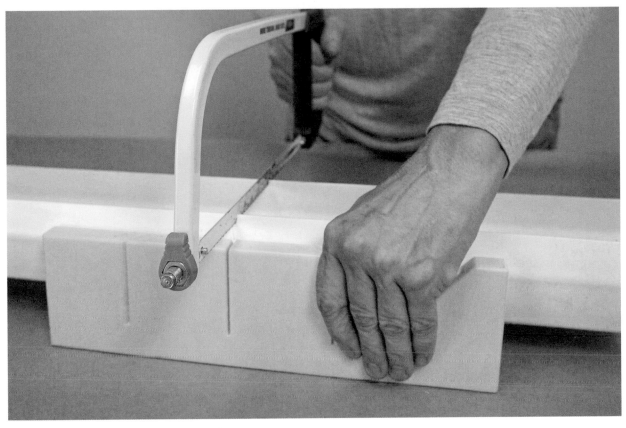

Saw the gutter into six 24-inch-long sections.

4 CUT THE RAIN GUTTERS TO SIZE AND DRILL DRAIN HOLES.

Using the miter box and hacksaw, cut the rain gutter into six 24-inch sections. The hacksaw works better on the plastic than the handsaw, as it has a finer tooth. After all the sections are cut, turn them upside down and drill small drainage holes along the bottom with the ⅛-inch bit.

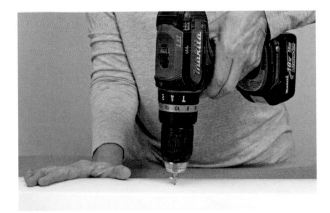

Drill a series of small drainage holes across bottom of the gutter.

5 MEASURE AND ATTACH GUTTER BRACKETS TO THE DOOR.

We used three planter boxes on each side of the door. You can hang them anywhere on the door as long as you leave less than 24 inches between brackets. Make sure the brackets line up horizontally, or your planters will be crooked. Before you screw the brackets into place, double-check your measurements from the top and the bottom to ensure they are even. Once the brackets are in place, snap or slide in the gutters, and attach the end caps. Add a little dirt and some colorful flowers or edible plants, and your green screen is ready to do its job.

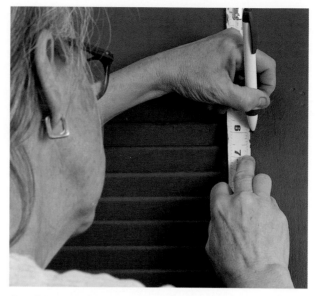

Carefully measure and mark bracket placement to ensure your planters will be even.

YOU CAN ALSO paint the gutters. If you decide to do this, use spray paint, which looks much cleaner on the plastic surface. Paint these when you are painting the door and support pieces. Rough up the exterior of the gutters with 100 grit sandpaper before you paint; this helps the paint adhere to the smooth surface of the plastic.

Screw in all the brackets.

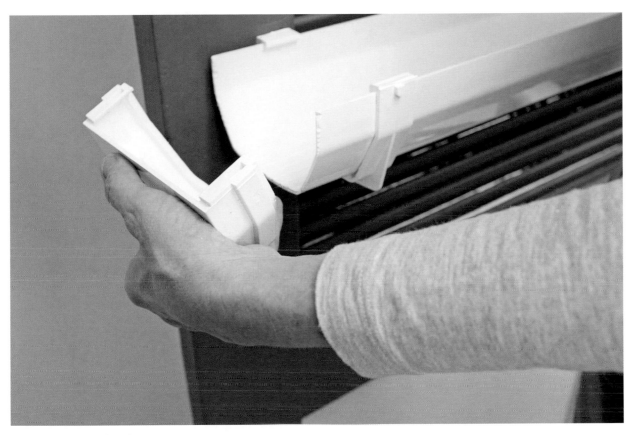

Snap in gutters and end caps.

No one would ever suspect this lovely entryway planter was once a common garbage can.

TRASH CHIC

Revamp a simple plastic garbage can with stencils.

———

This project is a real Cinderella story. You can transform anything with a good coat of paint and a little imagination, so we took a simple garbage can and used stencils to elevate it to a planter worthy of any front door. There are so many choices of stencils on the market today that your only problem will be deciding which one to use.

Materials and tools for creating a weighted bottom.

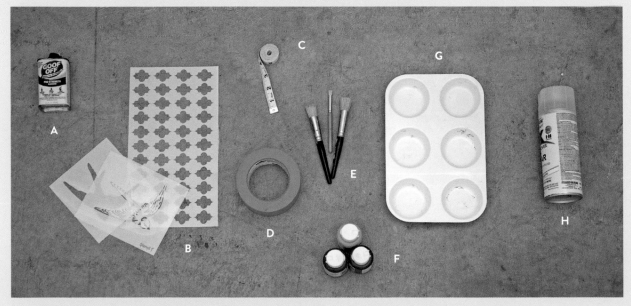

Materials and tools for creating the stencil design.

TOOLS & MATERIALS

WEIGHTED BOTTOM

A. Plastic garbage can

B. 1-in. PVC pipe

C. PVC cutting tool

D. Drill

E. 1-in. hole-saw drill bit

F. Plastic sheet

G. Protective gloves

H. Stirring stick

I. Concrete mix

J. Mixing bucket

Painter's tape (not pictured)

STENCIL DESIGN

A. Adhesive remover

B. Stencil

C. Measuring tape

D. Painter's tape

E. Stencil brushes

F. Acrylic paint

G. Paint tray

H. Clear sealer

Chalk (not pictured)

PREPARING

Choose your stencil, and then find the most accommodating container on which to place it. We purchased our stencil from a craft store. It was originally intended for a pillow, but with a few modifications (which we'll show you later) we made it work. We bought the garbage can from the cleaning department at a home-improvement store. It was almost a perfect cylinder, so it was easier to wrap the stencil around it (there are challenges when you try to curve something that was meant to be flat).

You can also make a weighted bottom for your planter. This step is not necessary, but it will give you a more substantial container that will not be blown or knocked over easily.

1 CREATE A DRAINAGE HOLE.

Begin by creating drainage for your container. Attach the hole-saw to the drill and make a hole right in the center of the bottom of the garbage can. This will happen very quickly, as a hole-saw bit is designed to go through at least 1 inch of wood and you'll be drilling through a small piece of plastic.

The 1-inch PVC pipe will serve as your drain through the weighted bottom. Cut the pipe to the desired length with your PVC pipe cutter. The length of the pipe equals the depth of the cement you will pour, so don't make it too long or your planter will be very heavy; 4 to 5 inches will suffice.

Drill your drainage hole.

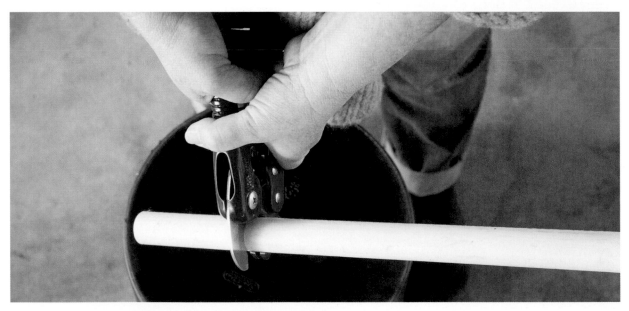

Cut the PVC tubing that will become the drainage hole.

Use tape to secure your PVC pipe.

Before you place the PVC pipe into the drainage hole, use painter's tape to cover the top so no concrete will pour through when it is in place. Make an X with two pieces of painter's tape, then place the bottom of the PVC pipe in the center of the X. This tape will help keep the pipe in place when you pour and will minimize the amount of concrete that could leak out from the bottom. Place the PVC pipe through the drainage hole, making sure the painter's tape adheres to the bottom of the garbage can. Turn over the garbage can, and place it on a plastic sheet to protect your work area. (It's very easy to separate concrete from plastic, but difficult to clean it off other surfaces.)

The tape will also help with leakage.

2 PREPARE AND POUR THE CONCRETE.

Fill about one third of a clean mixing bucket with the concrete mix. Work in a well-ventilated area, and do this slowly so you don't create undue dust. Cement dust is toxic, so use a mask if you have breathing issues or if you want to be cautious. Put on gloves, and slowly add water and stir until your mixture has the consistency of heavy cake batter. When your mix is the right consistency, immediately pour it into the garbage can, taking care not to go past the top of the PVC pipe.

If you did not make enough concrete to reach the top edge of the PVC pipe, mix more and add it until you do. Be sure the pipe and the concrete are even; if they are not, water could collect and rot the roots of your plant. Allow the concrete to set up at least overnight before proceeding.

If you add too much water to the concrete, pour in more mix to stiffen it up.

Add the concrete mixture until it reaches the top of the PVC drainage pipe.

Mark the garbage can all the way around so you have a guide.

Use your chalk lines as a guide to tape the stencil onto the can.

3 PAINT ON THE STENCIL.

Clean the garbage can completely. Remove any labels or price tags by rubbing hard with a rag and a few drops of adhesive remover. The entire surface should be smooth and clean.

Use a measuring tape and chalk to mark off every few inches where you want the top of the stencil to be. Do this around the entire garbage can.

Following the chalk guide lines, tape to the stencil to the garbage can, making sure it lies flat. Most containers are not perfectly cylindrical (ours wasn't), so cut the stencil as needed and make micro adjustments every few rows to ensure that it remains straight. (We cut our stencil to only three rows.) Pour your paint into the tray and dip your stencil brush in to lightly coat the bottom. Begin stenciling.

> **STENCIL BRUSHES** are different than normal paintbrushes. They are meant to be dabbed as opposed to brushed, which is why they have a thick, wide bottom. If you've never used one before, practice on paper to get the hang of it. Use just a little paint at a time (or blot before you begin) to prevent excess from seeping under the stencil.

Be careful not to put tape on your freshly painted stencil, as it will be easily pulled off.

When you have finished the first three rows, allow them to dry to the touch, then place the first row of stencil on the last row you just painted to use as your spacing guide. If you keep to this guide exactly, your top line will be off, so tilt the bottom of the stencil slightly away from your existing work so the top con- tinues evenly along your chalk guideline. After the border has dried, use the same dabbing technique for any additional stencils. If you are stenciling over existing work, hold the second stencil with your hand. Do not tape over exist- ing work, or the tape will pull it up.

4 SEAL YOUR WORK.

Normally when you're painting on a smooth surface you would rough it up with sandpaper or steel wool to give the paint something to stick to. Because this project uses the original color of the garbage can as the background, the surface is not prepared, so it is very important to spray a sealer on the container to preserve the stencil work. Use this sealer as you would any other spray paint, and take care not to hold the can too close so you don't create drips. Follow the sealer manufacturer's instructions for dry time before proceeding. Your stenciled planter is now finished and ready for its close-up.

You can spruce up everyday galvanized metal with spray paint and a water garden.

METALS

Metal comes in many forms, including aluminum, iron, and stainless steel. Every type has a different use and cost. Aluminum is light and will not rust, but its finish can be dull and it is not easy to manipulate. Stainless steel keeps its beautifully modern finish indefinitely, but it is quite expensive. Iron is easy to work with and looks wonderful with a patina, but exposure to the elements will cause it to rust. Lucky for us, there are many premade metal items that are already so close to being planters, they practically make themselves.

Who would guess that these chic hanging planters are a reimagined building material?

THE GABLES

Attic gable vents do double duty as a vertical garden.

We love when a client presents us with an unadorned wall. A blank canvas is a great opportunity. In this garden, the homeowners asked for a strong statement but didn't want to overpower the tranquil, Zen-like feeling of their outdoor dining room. We were reminded of an installation we did at an art gallery with our City Planters, and we decided to replicate it with a DIY twist.

Home-improvement and building-supply stores are two of our favorite places to roam around and get ideas. During one of these trips we came across gable vents, which are installed in home attics to allow air to pass through. We were stunned at their resemblance to vertical planters, and with just a few modifications, they were perfect for this purpose.

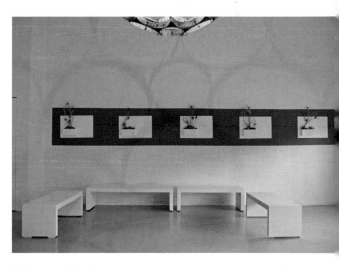

Using our City Planters in simple repetition provides the connection between the bold color blocking and the neutrality of this gallery space.

TOOLS & MATERIALS

A. Powder-coated metal gable vent

B. Ruler

C. Permanent marker

D. Drill with ⅛-in.-dia. metal drill bit

E. Wire spool

F. Needle-nose pliers with wire cutter

G. Plastic sheet

H. Medium grit sandpaper

I. Scissors

J. Caulking gun

K. Waterproof adhesive

For this space, we went with the rule-of-three design principle, which holds that objects grouped in odd numbers are more attractive and memorable than even-numbered combinations. We didn't have to do anything about color, as these vent gables are already powder-coated white, which was the perfect complement for the succulent-filled white Bauer canoe on the table. If white doesn't work for your installation, you can spray-paint the vents any color you want.

1 CREATE DRAINAGE HOLES.

Use a ruler and marker to measure the locations for five small, evenly spaced holes across the bottom of the vent, toward the front. Drill the holes.

Five holes allow for even drainage.

The holes are positioned toward the front of the planter, allowing water to drain away from the wall.

Measure and cut the wire for hanging.

Create a stop at one end by wrapping it around the pliers.

2 CREATE THE PLANT HANGER.

Gable vents are meant to be nailed into a wooden frame, so you will need to make a wire hanger for the back of the planter.

Measure and cut a length of wire at least 12 inches long. Pinch one end of the wire with the tip of the needle-nose pliers and coil the wire around the outside of the tip three times to create a stop. Loosen the pliers' grip and release the curled wire. Pinch the coiled tip flat, and bend the wire over the tool so it is at a right angle.

Thread the straight end of the wire through the top front of the planter. Pull the wire across, then thread it from the back to the front of the planter. Curl and pinch the coil as you did on the other end.

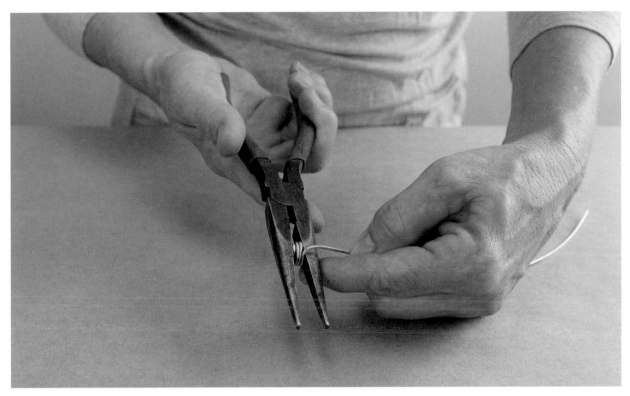

Pinch the coil flat with the pliers.

Pull the wire through one side until the coil stops it.

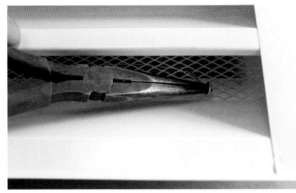

Create another coil on the other side to finish the hanger.

3 ATTACH PLASTIC BACKING.

The back of the vent is open mesh, so you will need to cover it with waterproof material to protect the surface on which you're mounting it and keep dirt from falling out of the back. Any plastic will do, and inexpensive placemats work great. Measure and cut the plastic back panel so it covers the entire back just below your newly created hanger.

Lightly sand the three back edges of the planter back and the plastic backing. The rougher surfaces will help give the adhesive a stronger bond.

Use the caulking gun to apply a thin line of adhesive all the way around the back of the planter, starting and finishing just below the wire hanger.

Guide the backing down gently and press evenly all the way around the frame. This will flatten the adhesive, remove any air pockets, and give you an even bond. Turn it over to dry so the weight of the metal helps with adhesion. Follow the adhesive manufacturer's instructions for dry time before proceeding.

Hang the planter as you would a picture frame; we used nails on wood. These reimagined gable vents are a perfect example of thinking outside the box and using imagination. This is one of the reasons DIY is so rewarding.

Measure and cut your plastic backing to size.

Rough up the metal and the plastic edges with sandpaper.

Apply a line of adhesive.

Place the sanded side of the back onto the frame of the planter.

The finished back.

Silver dichondra and yellow sundrops really pop against the planter's bright white background.

WE RECOMMEND using clear picture-frame rubber bumpers on the back of all wall planters. They provide a little friction to keep the planters from becoming crooked, and they get the planter further off the wall to keep moisture from being trapped and possibly damaging the wall.

A coat of copper spray paint helps this common stock tank add warmth and drama to a backyard.

STOCK TANK WATER GARDEN

Just add water—the magic ingredient in any garden.

———

Be it a birdbath, fountain, or a water garden, no outdoor sanctuary is complete without a water feature. It speaks to us on a basic, primordial level. It is the beginning of all life. Water attracts butterflies, birds, and dragonflies to the garden, and dappled sun on the water adds sparkle. A water feature of any size makes a big impact on the overall design of an outdoor living space.

Our friend Jules has a lovely bohemian cottage. Her house is petite and she spends a lot of time in the garden. The secluded yard has an enchanting outdoor dining area nestled into garden beds and fruit trees, but we all agreed something was missing—a water feature.

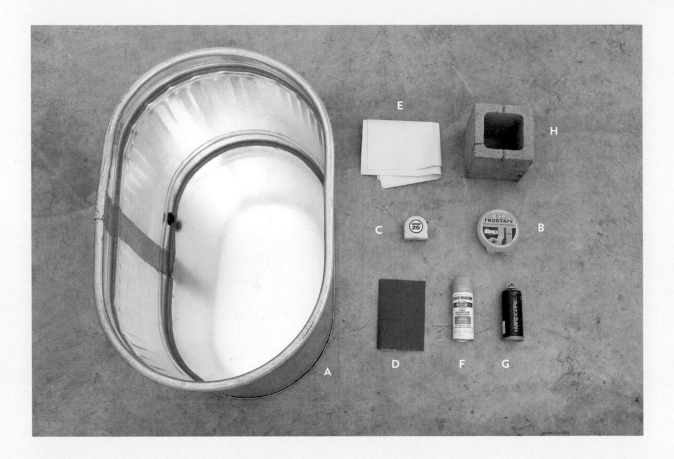

TOOLS & MATERIALS

A. 4 × 2 × 2-ft. stock tank
(purchase at feed stores
or online)

B. Painter's tape

C. Measuring tape

D. 120 to 180 fine grit
sandpaper

E. Plain newsprint

F. Primer spray paint

G. Copper spray paint

H. Cinderblock

First, decide how best to customize your container for its garden. Consider playing colors off one another or bringing in pops of hue. Jules wanted something funky to reflect her eclectic style and highlight the Latin-inspired color palette, so we opted for a warm copper.

1 TAPE OFF PAINT LINES.

To create a two-tone paint job, mask off the areas of the tank you won't be painting. First, decide where you want to paint. We used the natural ridges on the tank as our guides. If your tank doesn't have ridges, simply measure from the top and mark every few inches to ensure a straight line. Then go around the tank slowly with painter's tape, pressing the tape down firmly as you work. Do the same for the bottom edge.

2 SAND THE AREA BEING PAINTED.

Lightly sand the entire surface that will be painted so the paint will adhere to the metal.

Create the top edge of your spray line.

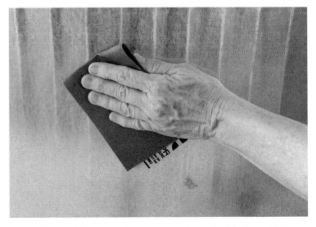

Sand the metal to create a greater bond with the paint.

3 MASK OFF THE AREAS THAT WON'T BE PAINTED.

Just below the first paint line, begin taping newsprint around the bottom and top areas that will not be painted. Be sure there are no gaps and that the seal is snug so there will be no overspray on the unpainted spaces.

4 SPRAY ON PRIMER.

In a well-ventilated area, spray one light, even coat of primer. Stay far enough away from the tank that the paint doesn't go on thick and cause drip marks. Follow the primer manufacturer's instructions for dry time before proceeding.

IF DRIP MARKS DO OCCUR on the primer or finishing coat, wait until the surface is completely dry, then gently go over the drip with a fresh piece of fine grit sandpaper to remove it. Lightly respray the repaired area.

Mask off the bottom of the tank.

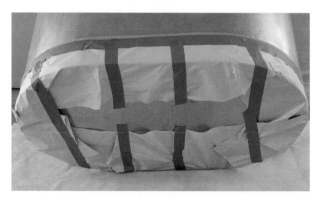

The tank is fully masked and ready for paint.

Apply one even coat of primer.

5 SPRAY-PAINT THE TANK.

In the same well-ventilated area, spray the paint onto the primed tank. As with the primer, spray lightly—it is better to underspray and repaint than to spray too thickly and have drip marks. Use two coats to get an even effect. Allow the first coat to dry to the touch before applying the second. Remove the newsprint and the tape as soon as the paint is dry to the touch. If you wait too long, the tape may pull off the dried paint. Place the cinderblock in the trough as a stand for positioning the plants. Now kick back and enjoy the tranquility your new water garden brings. It's magical!

Apply two even coats of the spray paint.

Allow the tank to dry completely before filling with plants and water.

Stenciled paint cans with grasses
bring a little bling to this garden.

HANGING AROUND WITH CANS

Create fetching wall planters with stenciled paint cans.

———

Wall planters are all the rage these days. They bring greenery into spaces too small for traditional pots and brighten up a wall with living art. They are available in many forms—felted wall pockets, wooden frames with sphagnum moss, plastic grids that lock together—and are often quite expensive. We wanted to create our own wall planters that were simple to make, cost effective, and amazing to behold.

Many of us already repurpose old cans into planters, but when we saw several nailed to a wall, we were inspired by the repetition and geometry they created en masse. Old cans are often hard to source, but new empty paint cans fit the bill. Hardware and paint stores carry these in one-gallon and one-quart sizes. Either works, but we chose the larger because we had a big wall to fill. We also like new cans because they are easier to work with, but used ones are fine as long as they are clean and have no toxic residue.

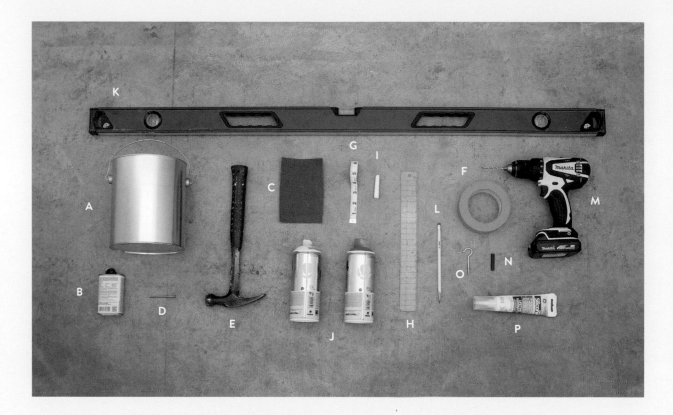

TOOLS & MATERIALS

A. Clean paint cans

B. Adhesive remover

C. 100 grit or higher sandpaper

D. ⅛-in.-thick nail

E. Hammer

F. Painter's tape

G. Measuring tape

H. Straight ruler

I. Chalk

J. Spray paint

K. Level

L. Pencil

M. Drill and appropriate bit
(for masonry or wood)

N. Anchors (if using
with a masonry wall)

O. #8 screw hooks

P. Silicone caulk

Primer
(optional; not pictured)

Before you begin, decide where to place your new wall hanging. This will help you figure out how many cans you need and determine your design. The yard we worked in is overshadowed by the neighbor's garage, so this project was the perfect way to give the wall some character and make it a part of the garden.

While considering the design, we went through our Tile & Pattern board on Pinterest until we came across a Moroccan floor pattern that we loved. Thinking of each can as a tile helped us visualize how we might achieve the same overall graphic effect with the alternating colors. We used painter's tape to create the stencil to shape the pattern on each can. You could also use a ready-made stencil or do a checkerboard or multicolor effect by painting each can a different color. We chose a blue-and-yellow combination because the house had the same blue on its trim and the garden was full of blooming yellow flowers.

Our inspiration tile from Marrakech Design of Sweden.

1 CREATE YOUR PATTERN.

We chose an alternating triangle pattern that we created by using tape as a stencil. On every other can the triangle points up or down and the stripe is blue or yellow. Make a guide by drawing the entire pattern on a sheet of paper, marking the colors and how many cans you'll need for each one so you don't get confused later (because believe us, you will).

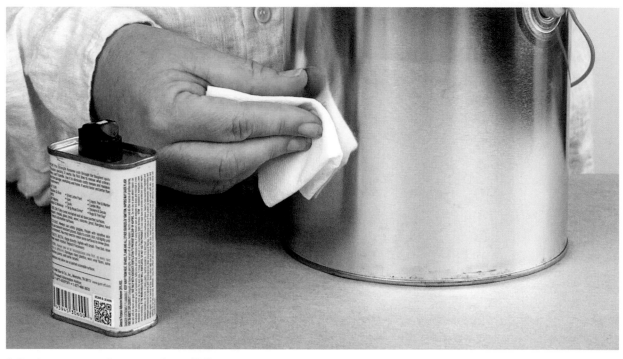

Adhesive remover cleans cans beautifully.

2 PREPARE THE SURFACE OF THE CANS.

Clean the cans completely. Remove any labels or
price tags by rubbing hard with a rag and a few
drops of adhesive remover. Make sure no residue remains, as anything left on the can will mar
the surface of the paint.

Lightly sand the cans, then wipe them
down. When the cans' surface is no longer
shiny, they are ready for painting. We chose
self-priming spray paint. If your paint is not
self-priming, apply a primer to give your paint
better coverage and durability. Follow the paint
(or primer) manufacturer's instructions for dry
time before proceeding.

Sand the whole can before you spray-paint.

It might take two or three strikes with the hammer until the nail goes through.

Don't be afraid to make several holes.

3 CREATE DRAINAGE HOLES.

You can make drainage holes with a drill, but it's easier to use a nail and hammer. Pound several holes in the bottom of the can.

Spray half the can with your stripe color.

Mark the center point with chalk.

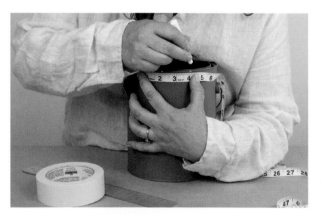
Mark the distance between your two stripes.

4 APPLY THE STENCIL AND SPRAY PAINT.

Paint one side of the can with the color that is going underneath the tape. Spray a wide enough area that you don't come up short when the tape goes on. Follow the paint manufacturer's instructions for dry time before proceeding.

Use the measuring tape to find the exact center between the handles of the can, and mark it with the chalk. Using that center point as your guide, decide what distance you want between your tape lines, and mark those with the chalk. Use the straight ruler to give yourself the same center point on the bottom of the can.

Using the chalk marks as your guide, apply the tape, taking care to smooth out any bubbles or wrinkles. When the tape is firmly in place, spray the entire can with the alternating color. Don't forget to paint the handle. Follow the paint manufacturer's instructions for dry time before proceeding. Continue this process for all your cans.

Apply the tape for the stripes.

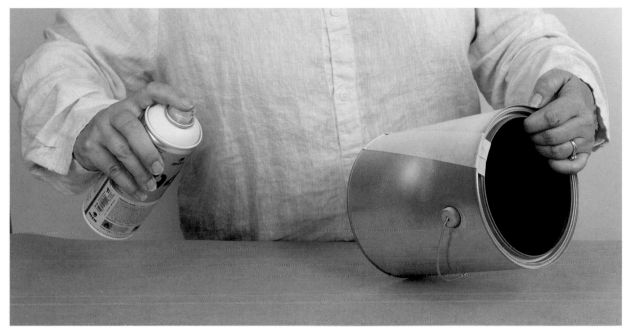

Spray the entire can with the alternating color.

5 REMOVE THE TAPE.

When the paint is completely dry, pull up the tape. The first color you applied will be the stripe and the second color will be the main color of the can.

6 PLANT AND HANG THE PLANTERS.

Plant your cans before you hang them. This will help you determine spacing, and it's much easier to plant something on a potting bench than it is on a wall. We used grasses because we love the way they sprout up from the top of the planter like hair. The planters alternate in color, so we decided to alternate the grasses as well.

We planted blue cans with blue fescue and yellow cans with 'Silver Dragon' lilyturf.

Use a level to ensure your cans are straight.

Predrill a hole for each hook.

Once the cans are planted, it's time to hang them on the screw hooks. You need to know how tall (or how long) your plant will grow so you can account for it when determining the distance between the planters. You will be very sad if your cans are covered with plants in a couple of months. The plant label is a good resource for this information, or you can check online.

Use the level to make sure you are hanging the cans on a straight line, and mark with pencil where you will drill. Whether working with masonry, stucco, or wood, predrill your holes using the correct drill bit for the surface. For masonry or stucco, the hole should be the correct size for the anchor; for wood, it should be slightly smaller than the hook. If using an anchor, pound it into the predrilled hole with the hammer. Twist in the screw hook and as far as it will go, with the open side facing up. If you are hanging the cans on a masonry or stucco wall, seal the area around each anchor with silicone caulk so water doesn't leak into the building through the opening (this isn't necessary if you are installing on wood). You are now ready to hang your planters and enjoy your beautiful new wall.

AS WITH ALL METAL, these cans will eventually rust through. To extend their life, spray a waterproof sealer on the inside of each can. Make sure it has fully dried before you add plants.

Use an anchor on a stucco wall and pound it in all the way.

Hang the planters.

Screw in the hook.

With a stucco or masonry wall, seal the area around each anchor to prevent water from running inside the wall.

1804

Salad bowls filled with 'Plum Pudding' heuchera look like flying saucers in this entryway garden.

FLYING SAUCER PLANTERS

These out-of-this-world containers are repurposed industrial salad bowls.

From the moment we first saw this project—created by our good friend and blogger Loree Bohl—we knew we wanted to do something similar. Loree was inspired by some amazing rusted metal dishes she spied during a garden tour. Knowing she could never afford the custom-made metal pieces, she decided to make her own version with bird feeders she found in a Portland feed store. We were excited to try this approach, but we simply could not find the right feeders. Finally we realized the feeders reminded us of industrial salad bowls, which are very inexpensive, readily available in restaurant supply stores or online, and made of super durable stainless steel. Problem solved.

Loree's flying saucers in her garden in Portland, Oregon.

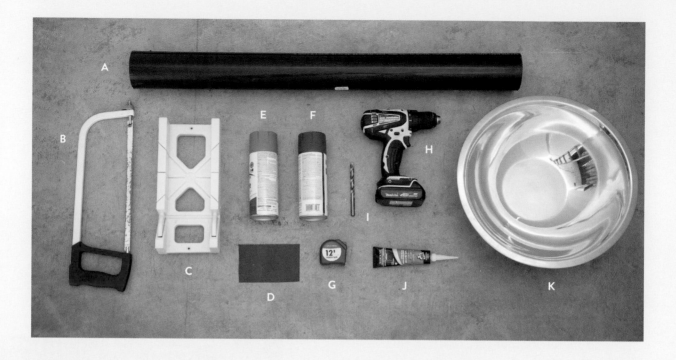

TOOLS & MATERIALS

A. 10-ft. length of 3-in. PVC pipe

B. Hacksaw

C. Miter box

D. 100 grit sandpaper

E. Primer

F. Spray paint

G. Measuring tape

H. Drill

I. ½-in. drill bit

J. Waterproof adhesive

K. 14-in. stainless steel salad bowls

PREPARING

First, decide how many planters you want to create. The rule-of-three design principle worked perfectly for our installation, as three staggered heights looks very interesting and creates a complete look near this modern entryway. Next, you must determine where they will live. Underplantings in the 12- to 24-inch height range work nicely, and also set off the space-age quality of the planters, helping them look like they are hovering. Loree used metal pipes to fly her saucers, but we thought PVC would be less expensive and easier to work with. We painted the pipes the same dark gray of the home's rain gutters to tie everything together.

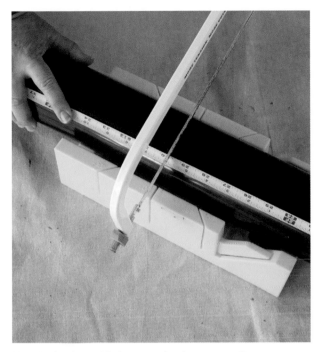

Use the hacksaw blade to mark where you will cut.

Cut all your pipe to length at the same time.

1 MEASURE AND CUT THE PVC TUBES.

Decide how high you want your saucers to soar. Remember to include the height of the bowls and to take into account how tall your plants will ultimately grow (if you are unsure, check the plant label or look online). Consider whether you will be blocking a window view or enhancing it. If you have a hard time visualizing the end result, try using bamboo sticks with cardboard glued on top to help you make choices. Once you've decided on the heights, add 6 inches to give yourself enough pipe in the ground for stability. Cut your PVC pipe to this length.

Place the PVC pipe in the miter box with your measuring tape alongside, and make a notch with your hacksaw at the correct measuring point. Saw a straight edge through the whole pipe. A new blade will work much more quickly than an old, dull one.

When sanding the tubes, don't forget to smooth out the rough spots the hacksaw created.

Prime plastic pipe before painting.

2 SAND AND PAINT THE PIPES.

Sand the entire length of each tube to rough up the surface so the paint will adhere better. Next, prime each tube. For best results, use a primer color that is closest to the end hue. For our project, gray was the perfect choice. When priming and spray-painting, make sure to hold your paint can at the recommended distance so you don't overspray and get drip marks. It is much easier to add a little more paint than to fix unsightly drips. Allow each tube to dry to the touch before proceeding with the next coat.

Spray-paint your final color once the primer is dry to the touch.

3 CREATE A DRAINAGE HOLE.

Using your drill and ½-inch bit, make a drainage hole directly in the center of each bowl. These bowls aren't too hard to drill, but if you have trouble, check the battery charge on your drill or try a new bit. A dull drill bit can be almost useless.

Drill a drainage hole in the center of each bowl.

4 ATTACH THE BOWL TO THE PVC PIPE.

Apply a good amount of adhesive to the top edge of the pipe. Lay the bowl top down on the ground, then attach the pipe exactly in the center of the bowl. Follow the adhesive manufacturer's instructions for dry time before proceeding. It is very important to let the adhesive dry completely, as this application has very little contact between the two pieces and you want as much strength as possible.

Once the pipe and bowl have dried, you can bury the pipes and add plantings. You could also bury the pipes before you attach the bowls and then glue them together in place. This version is the same as the upside-down one, except in reverse. After you have applied the adhesive to the top edge of the tube and placed the bowl on top of it, set a brick or a large stone in the bowl to help create a good bond between the two materials. No matter how you assemble your planter, make sure it is completely dry before you plant. Once planted, we guarantee you will get nothing but oohs and aahs from anyone who sees them. They are totally out of this world.

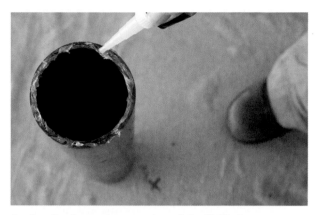

Apply adhesive to the top edge of the PVC pipe.

Leave the planter to dry with the weight of the pipe bearing down on the bowl.

Enamelware kitchen
bowls make striking
hanging planters.

KITCHENWARE
CONFIDENTIAL

Use traditional enamelware bowls as nontraditional hanging planters.

We have always loved the timeless, enduring design of speckled enamelware. It reminds us of camping, country living, and great flea markets. We combined this traditional cookware with stainless steel cable to create a fantastic modern hanging planter.

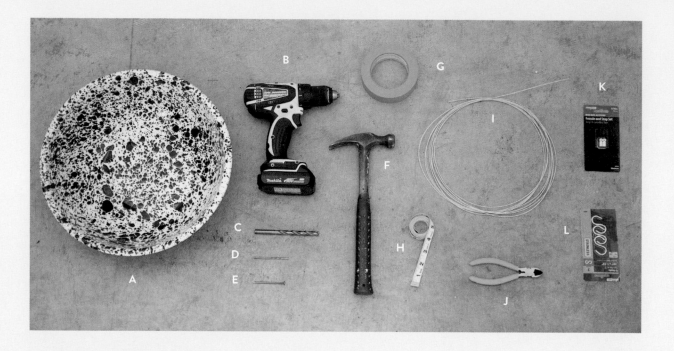

TOOLS & MATERIALS

A. 12- or 14-in. dia. enamelware bowl

B. Drill

C. ½-in. metal drill bit

D. ¹⁄₁₆-in. metal drill bit

E. ¹⁄₁₆-in. flathead nail

F. Hammer

G. Painter's tape

H. Measuring tape

I. ¹⁄₁₆-in. uncoated wire rope

J. Wire cutter

K. ¹⁄₁₆-in. ferrule and stop set

L. Stainless steel S hooks

The number of planters you are making will determine the hardware quantities you need to purchase. We wanted our hangers to be 18 inches long and we used three lengths per planter. We also needed extra length to make the loops, so we estimated 60 inches per planter for the wire length. You will also require three sets of ferrules and stops per planter. These come two to a packet, so you will use two packets for one planter.

STAINLESS STEEL WIRE rope makes excellent string to create different hanging lengths for your planters. Buy a few extra feet for this purpose. You will also need two ferrules to create the loop ends to attach to your ceiling hook and the top of the planter. Stops are not necessary.

You don't have to scour antique shops or raid your grandmother's attic to find good enamelware. It is still being produced and is available in many home goods or even sporting goods stores, and it's even easier to find online.

For planters, 12- to 14-inch serving bowls work best. (Salad bowls are too small to keep anything but succulents happy.) First, decide on color and quantity. We usually stick to the rule-of-three design principle, but in this case that would have been too many, as the space we were filling was quite narrow. A pair was the perfect choice. These planters are so striking that you might need only one.

Begin making your drainage hole with a hammer and nail.

Use the smaller drill bit to drill all the way through.

1 CREATE A DRAINAGE HOLE.

Enamelware is not easy to drill, so you will have to make a drainage hole in stages. First, hammer the flathead nail in the center of the bowl.

Put the ¹⁄₁₆ inch drill bit into the dent that the nail created. Press down hard until you get it to drill through.

Complete the hole with the ½-inch drill bit. You can also make several smaller holes, if that is easier.

The ½-inch drill bit should go through much more easily.

2 MEASURE WHERE TO PLACE YOUR HANGERS.

Three lines are perfect for creating a hanging planter. Two would make the container unbalanced, and four is more work and makes it harder to plant. Measure the circumference of the planter where the lines will attach, and divide by three. Use painter's tape to mark where the lines should go, and double-check that they are equidistant from one another. (It is easy to move tape, but not so easy to move a hole.)

3 CREATE HOLES TO ATTACH HANGERS.

Create the holes where you will run your hanging lines the same way you made the drainage hole, but without drilling the final ½-inch hole. First, create a dent in the enamel with the flathead nail.

Use the 1/16-inch drill bit in the mark to make a hole that goes all the way through. Do this on the edge of a table or on a raised piece of wood so you don't drill into your work surface.

Colored tape works well to mark drill points. Most permanent markers are difficult to see on the speckled enamelware, and the ink will be hard to remove.

Create a dent the same way you did for the drainage hole.

Drill the hole all the way through.

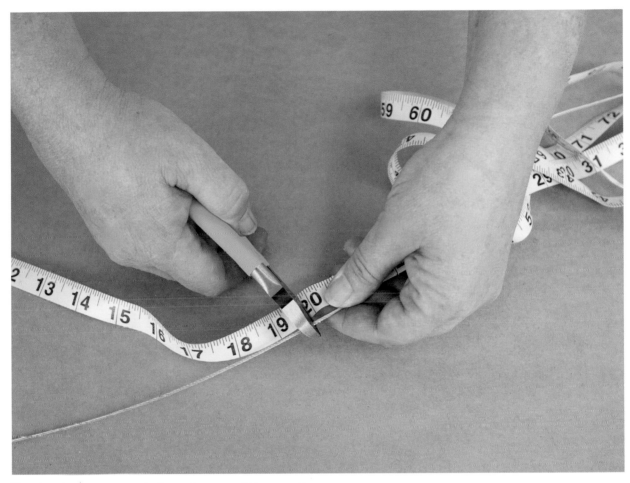

Use the wire cutters to cut all your hangers at the same time.

4 MEASURE AND CUT WIRE FOR HANGERS.

Cut all your wire at once. Use the measuring tape to create your first length, then use that piece as your pattern for cutting the rest. We wanted the lengths to be approximately 18 inches, so we cut 20-inch lengths and used the extra for our loops.

5 CREATE ALL THE LOOPS.

Use ferrules to create the loops. These little pieces of metal allow you to pull the wire through on one side, make a loop, and push the end through on the other side.

To secure the loop, use the hammer to pound the soft metal ferrule flat. This will cinch the wire and keep it from slipping. There are special crimping tools that will also do this, but a hammer works fine for this size wire and ferrule.

After you've made your first loop, measure it and make all the remaining loops the exact same size. It doesn't matter how you decide to measure (top of the loop, bottom or top of ferrule) as long as you do it the same way for every loop. If the loops are different sizes—even slightly—your planter will be unbalanced.

Push the wire through the ferrule to create a loop.

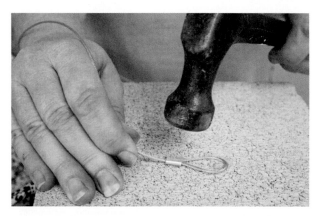

Flatten the ferrule with the hammer on something hard, like a concrete block, to flatten the metal from both sides.

Measure each loop to ensure they are all the exact same size so your planter hangs evenly when you put it together.

6 THREAD THE LINES AND SECURE THE ENDS.

Attach the lines to the planter. Thread the unlooped end of the wire down through each hole so the loop is on top. Thread the stop from your ferrule-and-stop set onto the end. Secure it the same way you made your loop. The enamel bowl is now ready to be planted. We used the traditional thrill-fill-spill method (something tall to catch the eye, something thick to fill in the top, and something long to cascade down). Once planted, gather the three loops together on one end of the S hook, and place the other end of the S hook onto whatever you are hanging it from. Stand back and admire a job well done.

A few hard pounds with the hammer will create a stop for the end of the hanger.

The hanger is securely attached to the planter, which will bear the weight of soil and plants when hung.

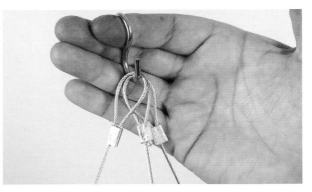

Use an S hook to gather the three loops together for hanging.

This sparkling centerpiece was once a humble building tool.

FRONT AND CENTER

A drywall mud pan finds new life as a dazzling centerpiece.

———

Great centerpiece containers are hard to find. After rectangular planters, they are the most-asked-for item in our store, so we decided to make our own. Because a centerpiece is always front and center, we knew it had to look amazing. Out of nowhere we realized there was a perfect solution—a drywall mud pan.

When a wall is being drywalled, after all the sheets have been screwed into place, the installer muds the wall to make it smooth. This involves applying several coats of the plaster-like mud over the entire surface with a trowel, sanding between each coat. The mud is applied from and scraped off into a rectangular box called a mud pan. Usually made from stainless or galvanized steel (and also available in plastic), these boxes are absolutely perfect as planters. We created a beautiful silver-and-gold planter; its shimmering surface and streamlined shape make for a gorgeous centerpiece.

TOOLS & MATERIALS

A. Stainless steel mud pan

B. Adhesive remover

C. Clean cloth

D. Glass cleaner

E. Painter's tape

F. 100 grit sandpaper

G. Butcher paper or plain newsprint

H. Primer

I. Spray paint

Measuring tape or ruler (not pictured)

You can find drywall mud pans at almost any hardware store. We fell in love with the stainless steel variety because we liked its modern shine, but you may prefer the galvanized ones, which will give you a more rustic look. The pans come in only a 12-inch length, but if you have a long table, consider using two or even three end to end to give you the coverage you need. Finally, decide whether the planter will live inside or outdoors to determine if you need drainage. If you do want drainage, use the technique from Flying Saucer Planters before proceeding.

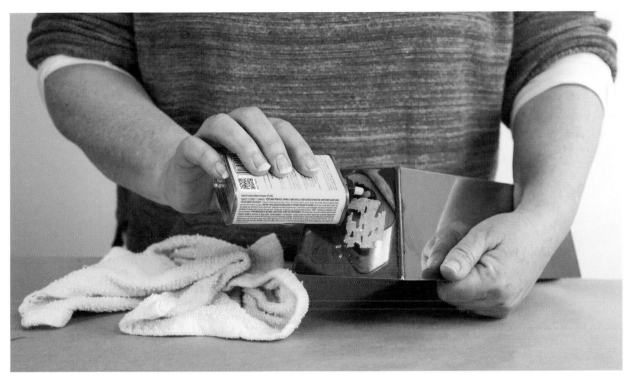

Use adhesive remover to take off any tags or stickers.

1 CLEAN THE SURFACE.

Clean the pan completely. Remove any labels or price tags by rubbing hard with a rag and a few drops of adhesive remover. Follow up with glass cleaner to eliminate any oils and smudges from the surface of the pan.

Glass cleaner does an excellent job of removing oil and smudges.

Decide how much area you want to paint, then tape off the rest.

Use a smaller piece of tape for the ends, being careful to line up the edges for a clean, professional effect.

Paper will finish the masking and ensure the spray paint goes only where you want it to.

2 TAPE OFF THE PLANTER.

Use painter's tape to mask off the areas around the pan that won't be painted. We wanted to create a gold-dipped effect by painting the bottom gold and leaving the top silver. Use one long piece of tape on each side, with smaller pieces for the ends. You can double-check with a ruler or measuring tape that the tape edge is the same distance from the top of the pan all the way around. Cover the entire not-to-be-painted area with butcher paper or plain newsprint to ensure it stays clean.

3 SAND AND PAINT THE PLANTER.

Use sandpaper to rough up the entire area to be painted so the paint will adhere better. Be very careful not to get too close to the tape edges. If you disturb the tape, the mistake will show up when you spray.

Next, prime and paint. You can skip the primer if you are using self-priming spray paint, but the gold paint worked much better on top of a coat of matte primer. The flat paint also provided better paint adhesion on the super shiny surface. When priming and spray-painting, make sure to hold your paint can at the recommended distance so you don't overspray and get drip marks. It is much easier to add a little more paint than to fix unsightly drips. Use one coat of primer and two coats of paint, and allow each coat to dry to the touch before proceeding with the next. Once you remove the tape, you will have the most chic centerpiece in the world. Throw a dinner party and enjoy it.

Sanding the shiny surface will help the paint adhere.

When painting over the primer, take care not to spray too long in one spot. Drippy paint would look terrible on this sleek container.

ALTHOUGH IT SEEMS logical that you should let everything dry completely before you pull off your masking tape, don't. You'll run the risk of the overspray drying to the tape, pulling off some of your hard work, and ruining the whole thing. Instead, pull off the tape only a couple of minutes after you have finished spraying. Leave your container to dry completely, resting on the unpainted edge.

The finished container reflects the pattern on the tablecloth in a very interesting way.

A terra-cotta chimney flue makes a perfect planter.

TERRA-COTTA

Terra-cotta pots are the most common containers around. The Italian versions can be quite expensive, but their quality is impeccable. Pots from Mexico and South America are prone to disintegrating quickly because of low firing temperatures in the kiln. The Asian versions, usually made in Vietnam, lack the refinement of their Italian cousins but are far superior in quality to those made in Mexico. Many building supplies are also made from good-quality terra-cotta, and some—like chimney flues—offer interesting new shapes. Most terra-cotta looks alike, but we have found a couple of ways to change things up.

The marbleizing on these pots makes them look extra special.

MARBLEIZED MASTERPIECES

Turn plain terra-cotta into a swirled work of art.

———

We fell in love with adorable little cups on Pinterest that had been marbleized and filled with Easter candy. They were made of plain plastic, but the marble-izing effect made them look much more elaborate. The method was so simple: pour three different paint colors into a tub of water, then roll the cups through it. We wanted to try the effect with larger containers.

After rolling countless terra-cotta pots through spray-painted water and getting questionable results, we decided this method was best for small proj-ects. But we were determined to find a way that allowed for greater coverage. After a bit of research, we finally perfected this slightly tricky painting style. It takes some practice, but it is well worth the trouble.

TOOLS & MATERIALS

A. Terra-cotta pot

B. Drop cloth

C. Primer

D. Plastic garbage can

E. Borax

F. Pot dipper (we used sprinkler parts)

G. Waterproof gloves

H. Three colors of oil-based paint

I. Turpentine

J. Newspaper

K. Sealer

Chopstick or pencil (not pictured)

Take a few practice runs before you attempt a larger container. We tested with 4-inch pots to see how the colors combined and to gain confidence. The paint that worked best was Testors Enamel Model Paint. It is inexpensive and available at most art-supply and craft stores, and usually comes in a package of several colors, so you can experiment until you come up with your favorite combinations. The pots we created were 12 inches and 16 inches; anything larger would have required a bigger dipping container than we could find (we used a 33-gallon plastic garbage can). But don't let that stop you, especially if you have a giant stock tank. Your dipping container must be big enough that you can completely submerge your pot.

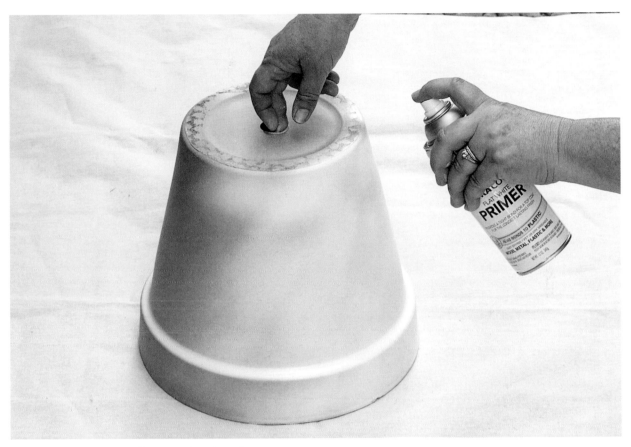

Protect your work area when spraying the primer.

1 PRIME THE CONTAINER.

Terra-cotta is porous, so it's best to give your pot a good coating of primer before you dip it in the paint. Protect your work area with a drop cloth. Turn the pot upside down, and prime it evenly all around. Let it dry for five minutes, then turn it over and prime the top edge and the top few inches inside the pot, which will likely still be visible after you add your plantings.

Mix the Borax well so it does not fall to the bottom of the dipping container.

2 PREPARE THE WATER.

Of all the things we learned while working on this project, the most important was correct water temperature. If your water is too cold, the paint coagulates and will not float on the surface. If it is too hot, the colors run together. You need tepid water, which is a little warmer than room temperature. It can be a challenge to get that much warm water outdoors, and we were glad our dipping container was on wheels. If you have a garage with a utility sink, you are golden. If not, keep adding pots of hot water from either your tap or a kettle until your water is the desired temperature. Also, do not set up your work area in the direct sunlight, as your paint will dry too quickly and you'll have to start again.

Once you have filled the dipping container with enough water to completely submerge your pot, add the Borax. This adds tension to the water surface and helps the paint float. You can create a marbleizing effect without using Borax, but we found that the swirls are not as clear and attractive. We used 2 cups of Borax with 30 gallons of water; you can adjust based on your own dipping container. Mix the Borax well. We created a combination mixing tool–pot dipper from one 36-inch length of PVC sprinkler pipe with one PVC tee threaded to the end to create a stop.

A PVC sprinkler riser with a tee screwed onto the bottom makes the perfect pot dipper.

3 PREPARE THE PAINT.

You are now ready to paint. Things will move pretty fast from this point forward, so make sure all your materials are ready and within reach.

Put on waterproof gloves. Thin all the paint before you add it to the water (if the paint is too thick, it will create a gloppy mess on the pot). Add a few drops of turpentine to the paint container, and shake it well.

Don't worry if a little turpentine spills into the water; this helps with mixing the paint.

All the paint should float on top of the water.

Blend the paint colors in the dipping container.

After thinning the paint, dribble it in a circular motion around your dipping container. Don't pour the paint in one spot, or you will have a hard time getting it to blend with the other colors. Add all three colors as quickly as you can, but don't rush.

After you have added all the paint, use a chopstick or a pencil to swirl the colors together gently. Stick the swirling tool in the center of any thick globs and gently pull them apart until none are left. Time is of the essence, because once your paint dries it won't adhere to the pot. The Borax and turpentine help extend your working time, but you have only two to three minutes. But don't worry: it's completely doable.

4 DIP THE POT.

Attach your pot to the dipper. Using two hands, hold the pot over the paint mixture. As you lower the pot, swirl it around so the paint creates movement.

Once the pot is fully submerged, leave it there for a moment. Hold the pot dipper with one hand and grab newspaper with the other. Use the paper to quickly pull off the paint that is starting to set up on the surface of the water. The paint will stick to the paper, and the top of the water should be fairly clean when you're done. Don't worry if you still have some haze.

Take the pot out of the water. Its shape will cause a vacuum to form, so tilt it at a slight angle.

Use two hands to help you twirl the pot down.

Place the pot right side up on your drop cloth and allow it to dry for at least 24 hours. Once the pot has dried, spray it with a clear matte sealer to prolong its longevity. When the sealer has dried, plant up your new pot like you would any other container.

Skim the paint film off the top of the water so you won't have ugly paint globs on your pot when you pull it out.

DON'T LET ALL your good Borax water go to waste. Use a kitchen skimmer to clean the water surface so you can begin again. There may be a little oily residue from the turpentine, but that's fine. You can even save it for another day—just add some hot water to bring it back to tepid.

After you pull the pot out of the dipping container, hold it for a few moments to let any excess water drip off.

The swirled yellow pots really complement the echeverias and aeoniums planted inside.

A painted chimney flue planter harmonizes colorfully with its tranquil background.

CHIM-CHIM CHER-EE FLUE PLANTER

Chimney flue liners have a wonderful shape for statement planters.

We were—as we often are—daydreaming in a building yard when we spotted pallets of clay chimney flue liners. Like magpies drawn to sparkly objects, we were attracted to this terra-cotta fireplace material because it was just begging to be turned into planters.

TOOLS & MATERIALS

A. Backer board

B. 18 × 11 × 12-in. clay chimney flue

C. Gloves

D. Safety glasses

E. Reciprocating saw (or jigsaw)

F. Backer board scoring knife

G. 100 grit sandpaper

H. Drill with ¼-in. masonry drill bit

I. Caulking gun

J. Waterproof caulking adhesive

K. Latex gloves

L. Metal measuring tape

M. Compass

N. Painter's tape

O. Pencil

P. Outdoor acrylic paint in black, orange, and cerulean blue

Q. Plastic paint cup

R. Paintbrushes: 1-in. for filling in; ¼-in. for fine edging work

S. Clear matte acrylic spray sealer

Our inspiration pottery from Pawena Studio.

PREPARING

Chimney flues are produced in a range of sizes and shapes. They are square, cylindrical, or oval, and many different heights and diameters. The most readily available ones are the 18-inch ovals, which you can find in many building material yards without special ordering.

The flues are nice terra-cotta and would be just fine as is, but we wanted to have some fun with them. We are smitten with the ceramic work of Pawena Thimaporn, and we wondered how her bold, abstract style might enhance the appeal of these already wonderful pieces. We reimagined a pattern from one of her tabletop cylinders for the larger oval format of the chimney flues. We hand-painted the design, and were thrilled with the results.

FOR MORE GRAPHIC inspiration and ideas for painting your own chimney flue planters, check out abstract artist Sophie Taeuber-Arp. A forerunner of the Dada art movement in the early 20th century, Taeuber-Arp holds the distinction of being the only woman ever featured on a 50-franc Swiss banknote.

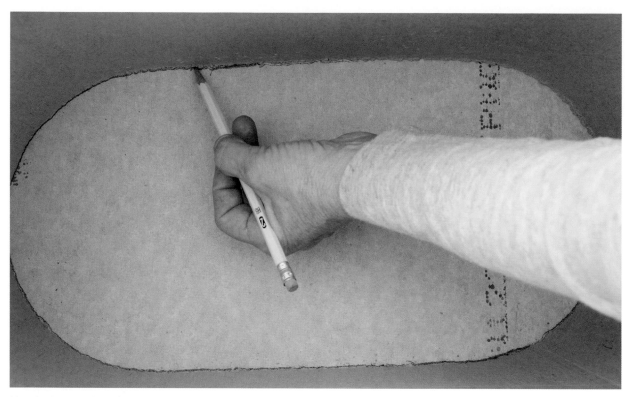

Use the inside of the flue to make a pattern on the backer board.

1 OUTLINE BACKER BOARD TO CREATE THE PLANTER BOTTOM.

Place the chimney flue on top of the backer board. Make one edge your starting point so you will have less to cut. Use the pencil to trace the inside of the flue, creating a pattern you can follow with the backer board knife and the reciprocating saw.

Use the scoring knife to make a groove in the backer board.

2 SCORE AND CUT THE BACKER BOARD.

Go around the pencil outline a few times with the scoring knife (see The Modern Rectangle for instructions on scoring). Move in small increments, steadily working your way around the entire pattern. Repeat this until the groove is about ⅛ inch deep. Scoring makes it much easier to stay on track with the power saw. We put the backer board on sawhorses to make cutting safer and easier.

When the groove is deep enough, use your reciprocating saw to finish cutting the pattern. Wear safety goggles and gloves.

Cut out the pattern with reciprocating saw.

3 CREATE DRAINAGE HOLES AND ATTACH THE BOTTOM.

Using the drill and masonry bit, make three holes in the backer board for drainage. Set it into the bottom of the flue to attach.

Push your cutout into the flue. If you have trouble getting it to fit, do a light sanding around the edges of the board to smooth any rough bits that could cause it to stick. When it is in place, wipe the edges to remove fine dust particles, which could weaken a strong adhesive bond. From the inside of the planter, use the caulking gun to slowly apply a line of adhesive all around the seam between the wall and the backer board bottom. With your latex-gloved index finger, smooth the adhesive and seal the area between the two materials. Follow the adhesive manufacturer's instructions for dry time before proceeding.

Drill drainage holes.

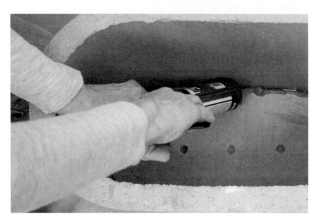

Attach the backer board to the inside of the flue with the adhesive caulking.

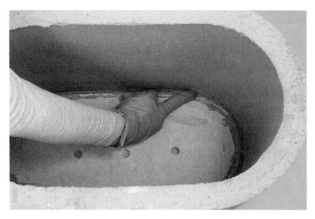

Use a gloved finger to push adhesive into cracks.

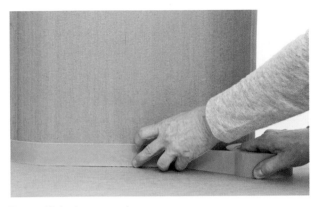
Tape off the bottom edge.

4 TAPE OFF THE EXTERIOR OF THE PLANTER AND PAINT THE ORANGE BAND.

Decide how large your orange band should be, and begin measuring and taping it off. We used the width of the painter's tape to give us our border along the bottom edge.

Measure and mark the top edge. Make small marks with the pencil all around the planter so your line is even. Tape off the top edge, taking care to follow the pencil marks so the band is the same width all the way around.

Using one of the larger paintbrushes, paint the band orange. Follow the paint manufacturer's instructions for dry time before proceeding.

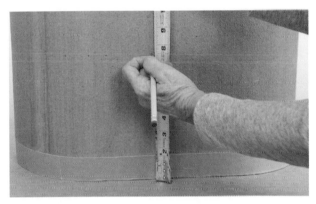
Mark the top edge of the orange band all the way around.

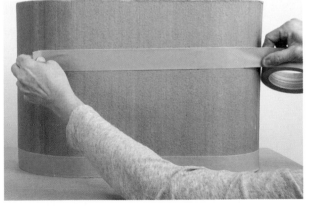
Tape off the top line.

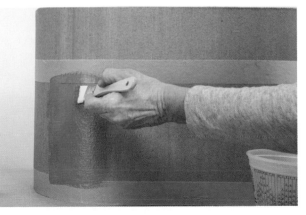
Paint the orange band.

5 CREATE THE BLUE HALF-CIRCLE.

Use the compass to draw the outline for the blue half-circle. Hold the compass point fixed in a single spot, which should be the middle point of the half-circle. Move from left to right with the other end, which will create the half-circle. Use a light hand: you want to see the outline clearly but keep it faint enough that it won't be visible once you paint it.

When painting the half-circle, use the smaller brushes to create the outline, then switch to larger brushes for the middle. It's too difficult to tape off the round shape, so to get a crisp edge, take your time, paint in small increments, and use a straight-edge brush, as pictured.

Use the compass to create an even half-circle.

Paint the blue half-circle.

6 TAPE OFF AND PAINT THE BLUE BAND AND THE BLACK MIDDLE AREA.

Tape downward from the side edge of the half-circle (where it meets the orange band) to the bottom of the container. It is important to keep this line straight. Do this on both sides of the half-circle. Next, tape off the blue band area below the orange. You will be taping on the orange paint. When you remove the tape after you paint the blue band, some orange might pull up. Minimize this by waiting until the orange paint is fully dry and removing the tape slowly. Touch up the orange paint as needed.

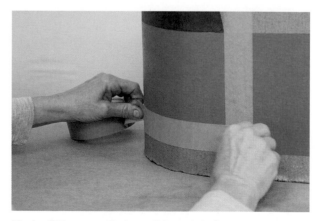

Mask off the areas that won't be painted.

Fill in the orange square area with black paint. There will be tape on the right and left. The top and bottom will be freehand, so use the smaller brush here. Paint the edge that meets the half round first, and then the black edge that meets the bottom blue band. Fill in the rest of the black area with a larger brush.

7 SEAL THE PLANTER.

Seal the paint to preserve all your hard work. We used matte spray-on sealer, but if you want a little shine, you could use a satin or semi-gloss. Gloss is so shiny and reflective that it can be distracting and hard to apply evenly; we do not recommend it. Choosing the design for these statement planters was a lot of fun. Finding inspiration and deciding on your palette really flexes the creative muscles.

Paint the bottom blue to match the top of the half-circle.

Paint in the black area to finish.

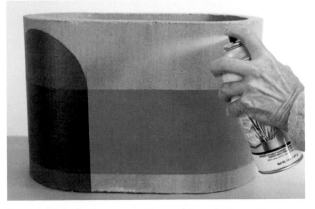

To give your work a longer life, seal the planter with clear matte spray paint.

Rope is one of the oldest organic building
materials still in use today.

ORGANIC MATERIALS

In a garden, organic materials will eventually decompose into the soil unless you provide consistent care and maintenance, but the extra effort is worthwhile. Natural objects have a textural and inviting quality that is hard to re-create in synthetic alternatives. Even with attention, they won't last forever—but they will be extra special for as long as they do.

Your wallpapered planter is truly one of a kind.

DECOUPAGE GOES OUTDOORS

Use a simple technique to make the most custom planter you can dream up.

Decoupage is Art 101: tear up or cut out paper, glue it to something, and cover it with varnish. Decoupage is not usually considered an option for outdoor planters, but with newer exterior glue products now available, the technique is full of possibilities for your garden.

We wanted to try decoupage because we love wallpaper, which has the ability to take the ordinary to the extraordinary. Wallpaper has the same appeal as tile, but you never see wallpaper outdoors. We decided to change that, and collected leftover scraps from one of our favorite wallpaper designers, Madison and Grow. We wanted to feature the beautiful paper as a cutout so it would stand out and we would need only a small amount. This fun and relatively easy project brings all sorts of possibilities to outdoor—or indoor—decor.

A beautifully wallpapered room is so inspirational.

TOOLS & MATERIALS

A. Container

B. Primer

C. Spray paint

D. Wallpaper

E. Scissors

F. Outdoor/exterior Mod Podge glue

G. Plastic cup

H. Foam brush

Waterproof enamel sealer
(optional, not pictured)

First, choose your planter. We picked a plastic pot, but you could use terra-cotta, metal, or glass. Next, find your wallpaper. Any type of paper is fine, but wallpaper tends to be printed on heavier paper, which is easier to work with and sturdier, and the patterns are large so you have the option of making a bigger statement. Plus, there are so many gorgeous styles from which to choose. If you aren't looking to spend extra money, perhaps you have (or a friend has) some leftover paper from a remodel. Or try our standard trick and buy samples from a show-room—you might even get them free. Many companies are online and will send you samples for a small fee.

Once you have your materials, experiment with how they play against each other. This will help you decide how much wallpaper to use. We chose a beautiful green paper with a vibrant gold line. The gold was the inspiration for painting the pot the same color and using the vertical quality of the design as a stripe down the middle.

1 PAINT THE PLANTER.

You will likely want to prime your container so the main color goes on easier. If you are using self-priming paint, you can skip this step. (If your container needs a drainage hole, drill it before you prime.) The planters we used had a slight texture, so we needed as much coverage as possible to help even out the surface so the paper would adhere better. Protect your work area with newspaper or a drop cloth. Follow the primer manufacturer's instructions for dry time before proceeding.

Spray-paint the container, taking care to cover it evenly. Start with the planter upside down to coat the underside well. After it has dried a bit, turn it over and paint the top, including the top few inches inside. If you need two coats, let the first application dry completely before applying the second.

Prime your container in a well-ventilated area.

Even though we used primer, we needed two coats to get even coverage of the gold color.

Good scissors come in handy for clean cutting.

Mod Podge comes out white but dries clear.

Foam brushes are disposable, so you don't have to worry about glue ruining a good brush.

2 DECOUPAGE THE PLANTER.

While your freshly painted container is drying, decide how you want to use the wallpaper, and then cut it accordingly. We wanted our paper to look like it was painted right on the surface, so we cut very close to the gold lines so they blended into our gold base coat.

Pour a small amount of Mod Podge into the plastic cup. Decanting the glue makes it easier to use and reduces the potential for contaminating the whole jar with lint or dirt that may catch in your brush as you work. In addition to its adhesive properties, Mod Podge is a sealer and a finish.

Using the foam brush, apply a generous amount of Mod Podge to the area you want the wallpaper to go. Apply the same amount to the back of the paper. If the glue feels too thick, dip your brush in water to thin it out.

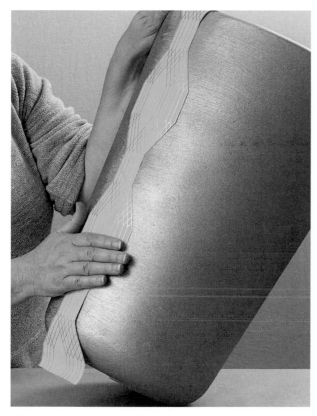

Mod Podge dries clear and is very forgiving.

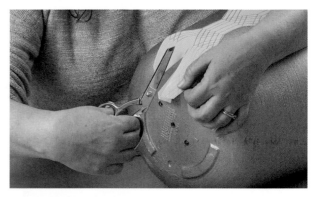

Be careful not to cut too high.

For the best adhesion, put glue on the planter and the paper.

Starting at the top of the pot, apply the paper. Do this slowly, smoothing it as you work your way down. Once the paper is applied, you can use a brayer (a small rolling device) to help remove any bubbles or wrinkles that may appear. (This wallpaper was thick and we used a small amount, so we didn't need one.) Don't worry if glue seeps out at the edges; just wipe off the excess with the damp foam brush. Mod Podge dries clear, so you won't have glue marks.

Once the main part of the paper is in place, curve it underneath the bottom of the con-tainer so it lies smoothly and disappears. Cut a slit in the paper up the middle until you get to the point where it curves. The paper will now be able to bend smoothly under the planter without puckering on the sides. Take care not to cut too high.

When you're satisfied with the angle of your cut and how the paper is laying, glue the paper to the bottom of the container. If you're doing both sides of the planter, repeat the pro-cess until you're happy with your layout.

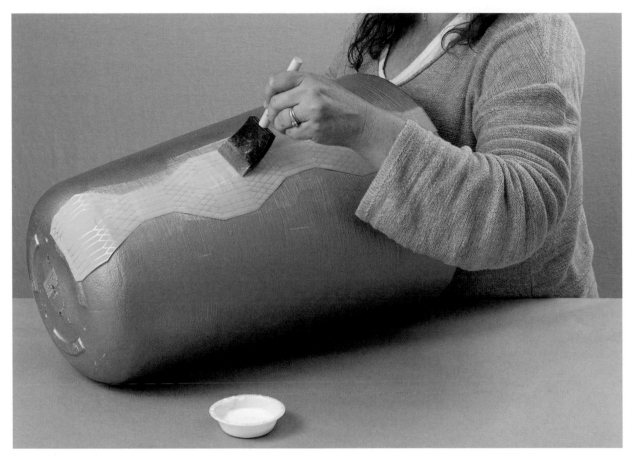

Be generous with your application and take the time to feather it out.

Mod Podge must dry between coats or it will get tacky and difficult to work with. Wait 15 to 20 minutes for it to dry, then coat the top of the design with glue. Cover your design with four to five coats, allowing no less than 15 minutes of drying time between coats. It's not necessary to coat the entire planter, as the Mod Podge dries with a matte finish and is invisible.

Mod Podge is weatherproof, but we recommend brushing on a final coat of waterproof enamel sealer if your planter is going to be in a very exposed area. (Our planter lives on a sheltered porch, so we felt it wasn't necessary.) Use the sealer on the entire planter, as most products have a little shine and you want your planter to have a consistent look. Follow the manufacturer's instructions for dry time before proceeding. Once the container is dry, plant it with your favorites. And be warned: you may want to start putting wallpaper on everything.

The final container planted with a braided weeping fig (*Ficus benjamina*).

An age-old tool gets a
modern makeover.

ROPED IN

Rustic modern cylinders work inside or outdoors.

———

Rope is one of the most tried and true DIY materials. In this project, we move away from its utilitarian past and into 21st-century decor with a handsome cylinder planter. We love pairing these textured garden planters with more conventional containers like terra-cotta and giving them a modern rustic quality. This simple idea requires only a few materials, is inexpensive and easy, and looks fantastic.

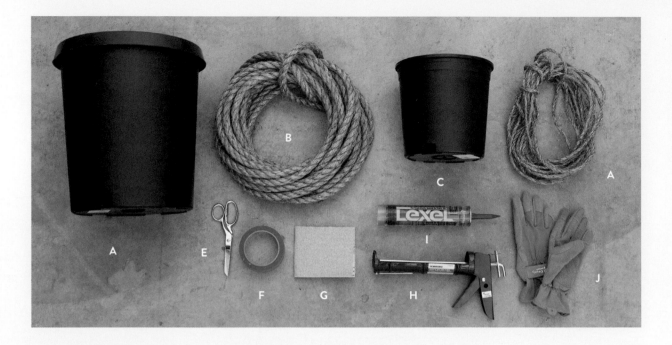

TOOLS & MATERIALS

A. 5-gal. black nursery container

B. ¾-in.-dia. jute rope

C. 2-gal. black nursery container

D. ¼-in.-dia. jute rope

E. Scissors

F. Painter's tape

G. Medium grit sandpaper

H. Caulking gun

I. Waterproof caulking adhesive

J. Gloves

In this Mediterranean-style location with a heavily carved wooden door and a rock path, we used natural jute rope in two sizes for rustic, textural contrast. You could also work with brightly colored rope, synthetic fibers, or both. For another effect, you can paint the rope or dip-dye the entire container.

TO CALCULATE how much rope you will need to wrap the container, divide the height of the pot by the width of the rope, then multiply the sum by the circumference of the container. Divide this sum by 12 to determine the number of feet of rope you will require. If your pot tapers, you will need slightly less.

1 PREPARE THE CONTAINER.

Sand the entire surface of the 5-gallon container until it is roughed up and no longer smooth. This will allow the adhesive and rope to get a good grip.

Use sandpaper on the entire container surface.

2 APPLY THE ROPE.

Cut the ¾-inch rope at an angle at its starting point. This creates more rope surface for the initial bonding of the materials and gives it a clean end.

Turn the container upside down. While wearing gloves, use the caulking gun to squeeze out a dime-size amount of caulking adhesive just under the rim, and press the angled end of the rope into it. This is the starting point. If the container does not have a rim, hold the angled end on the container ¼ inch from the top edge. The angled side of the rope should press into the sealant.

Angle cut the rope end for gluing.

Tuck the angled end under the rim.

Use the waterproof adhesive to bond the rope to the container.

Squeeze a thick line of adhesive around the pot, and begin wrapping the rope over it. Make sure the rope doesn't slip as you apply the sealant; it should be snug against the container.

Add another generous line of adhesive and wind another row of rope around the container. Keep each row of rope close to the previous one. Squeeze out another line of adhesive onto the pot and follow with the rope, smoothing and pushing each row close to the next. Continue in this manner until you reach the top.

Keep pushing the rope down.

Continue applying adhesive and following with rope.

Keep the rows tight and snug against the container.

Finishing the wrap.

Tape will hold the rope in place while the sealant dries.

3 COMPLETE THE WRAP.

When you reach the top, make the same angled cut from Step 1, followed by another thick application of adhesive to hold the end in place.

Use painter's tape to keep the rope secure while the adhesive dries (don't be afraid to use a lot of tape). Repeat the process with the 2-gallon container and ¼-inch rope. Allow the adhesive to dry completely before you use your new planters. Whether these planters live inside or outdoors, you'll find they bring an interesting textural element to your potted arrangements.

Textural variations create subtle points of interest on this driftwood planter.

CATCH MY DRIFT

Make a beautiful planter out of driftwood.

Over the years, we have seen many found objects turned into plant containers. Tires, old drawers, vintage coolers, colanders—the list goes on and on. But one of our favorite methods is to transform driftwood logs into gorgeous planters. These projects are fairly easy to create, and they never fail to impress, as every piece is unique. The hunt for the perfect specimen of driftwood is part of the pleasure. You don't have to live near the ocean to find these wonderfully weathered pieces. Creeks, lakes, and rivers have driftwood along their shores. A walk in the woods will usually turn up fallen tree branches, which will also work. Take a keen eye and a pair of gloves with you, and let the hunt begin. Make sure to choose old, dry wood, as green wood is difficult to work with.

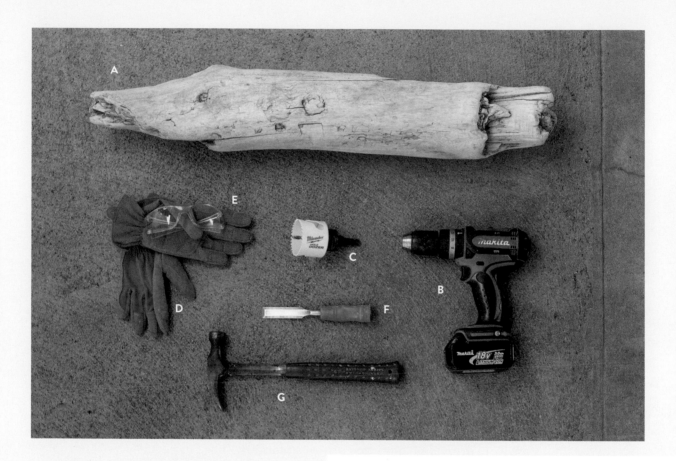

TOOLS & MATERIALS

A. Driftwood

B. Drill

C. 1½-in.-dia. hole-saw bit

D. Gloves

E. Protective eyewear

F. Chisel

G. Hammer

Driftwood planters make great flowerbed borders, table centerpieces, and even hanging planters. When looking for driftwood or fallen limbs, make sure the piece is deep enough for the plants you intend to use. Succulents have very shallow root systems, so they work well. If you choose driftwood from the ocean, clean it thoroughly before you use it. Salt is not a friend to plants.

1 DRILL OUT THE PLANTING AREA.

Before you do anything else, it is important to find out how the piece of wood naturally wants to rest. Lay it on a flat, firm surface so you can decide where to drill the planter trough. Once you know where you're going to drill, put on gloves and protective eyewear, attach the hole-saw bit, and begin drilling holes in a line so they barely overlap. A hole-saw bit is normally used to bore holes into a door for inserting a lock. Your wood will be thicker than a door, so the bit will create perfect round circles for you to chisel out.

2 CHISEL OUT THE WOOD CIRCLES.

Wedge the chisel tip edge down between each circle, and slowly angle the chisel upward. Some circles will pop out easily. For the tougher ones, angle the chisel toward the base of the circle and use the hammer to pound the end, which should loosen the circle. The side of the chisel with the angled edge faces what you are discarding. The angle helps to get underneath and loosen what you're trying to chisel out.

Use your foot to steady the wood as you bear down on the drill to create your first hole.

Drill a line of barely overlapping holes.

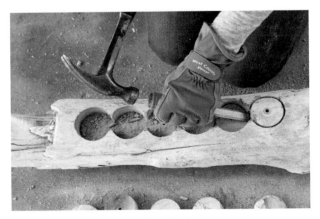

Chisel out the routed wooden circles.

A second pass with the drill will give you more planting depth.

Pound the chisel into the middle of the circle.

3 DO A SECOND ROUND OF DRILLING (IF NEEDED).

You will likely want to do a second pass with the drill to create a deeper planting bed. Use the drill to bear down into the existing holes and make them deeper.

This second round of drilling will be harder to remove. Position the chisel in the middle of the wood circle, then use the hammer to pound the chisel into the middle and split it.

While the chisel is buried in the center of the circle, gently rock the chisel back and forth to widen the split. One of the halves should release easily from the main body and come out.

Next, use the chisel as a wedge to separate what's left of the circle by pounding the end with the hammer until it separates. Repeat this with each hole. Use the chisel flat side down to remove bigger chunks of wood at the bottom that did not come out with the bulk of the circle halves.

Wiggle the chisel back and forth to split the wood.

Chisel out what's left of the circles.

Chisel out the inside ridges to finish the planter.

4 CHISEL OUT WOOD BITS BETWEEN THE CIRCLE HOLES.

To finish the planter, chisel out the pieces of wood created by the circle drillings. Make sure the angled side of the chisel faces the pieces being removed, and go down each side until all the ridges are gone. You could also add drainage holes, but they aren't necessary. The wood will absorb water and dry out on its own.

These unique planters are a perfect centerpiece for an outdoor dining or coffee table, and a sure-fire way to spark a conversation.

The finished planter ready for plants.

Hide an unsightly nursery pot with a custom fabric bucket you can coordinate with your decor.

FABRIC
BUCKET

Swap out your heavy
ceramic pots
for lightweight,
decorator-friendly
planter covers.

Want a plant container that matches the
sofa pillows? How about something fes-
tive for the holidays? Do you like changing
colors and accents to match the seasons?
With a fabric bucket you can do all this and
more. Plants will stay happy in their original
nursery containers, and you will love all the
options these easy-to-make buckets provide.

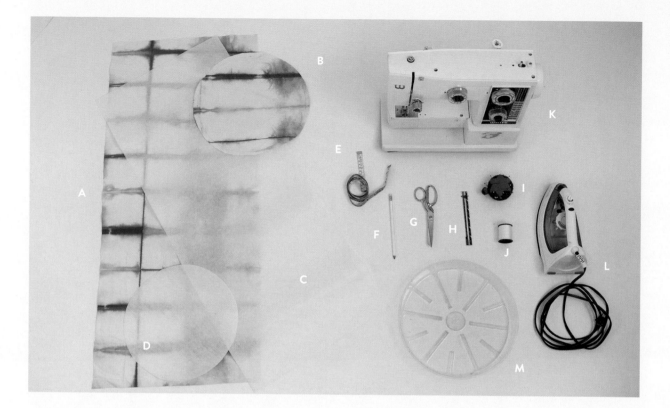

TOOLS & MATERIALS

A. Two pieces 40 × 17-in. fabric

B. Two pieces 13-in.-round fabric

C. One piece of 39 × 16-in. nonwoven fusible interfacing, medium to heavy weight

D. One piece of 12-in.-round nonwoven fusible interfacing, medium to heavy weight

E. Measuring tape

F. Pencil

G. Fabric scissors

H. Sewing gauge

I. Straight pins

J. Thread

K. Sewing machine

L. Iron

M. 12-in. plastic plant saucer

The indigo-dyed shibori drying in the sun at our workshop.

PREPARING

Shibori is the Japanese technique of binding fabric before dyeing it to achieve a variety of patterns. In the 1960s, American counterculture co-opted this technique to create tie-dye. Potted hosted a shibori workshop that featured indigo dye, and we thought it would be fun to create the pattern as well as the container. We took a few yards of heavyweight cotton canvas and played with an accordion wrap to achieve an interesting pattern. We fell in love with the results. The bucket we constructed is designed to fit a 5-gallon nursery container with a 12-inch plastic saucer for drainage.

You can create your own shibori or tie-dyed fabric, or visit a fabric store, which will provide many more choices of pattern and design. Look for sturdier textiles that can hold a shape, like canvas, upholstery fabrics, and outdoor materials.

1 CUT FABRIC AND INTERFACING TO SIZE.

Measure and cut your textile to the sizes specified in the materials list. Do the same for the interfacing, which will be 1 inch smaller than the fabric. Interfacing stiffens fabric and will give your container structure. The 12-inch plastic saucer is the perfect drainage size for a 5-gallon nursery container, and it has the added bonus of giving you a pattern for cutting your interfacing. The fabric cutouts must be 1 inch larger than the interfacing, so use the sewing gauge to mark the additional ½ inch all the way around to make the two 13-inch circles.

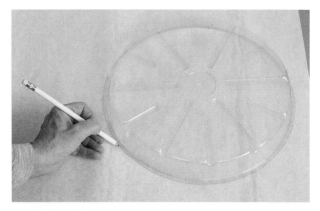

Turn the 12-inch plastic saucer upside down to its widest point to trace your pattern to cut the interfacing circle.

When cutting the fabric circles, use the sewing gauge to mark an additional ½ inch all the way around so the circles have a 13-inch diameter.

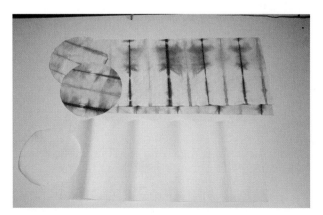

The cut fabric and interfacing.

2 FUSE THE INTERFACING TO THE FABRIC.

Use the iron to fuse the interfacing to the wrong side of one of the rectangles and one of the fabric circles. Follow the manufacturer's instructions for the interfacing.

Fuse the interfacing onto the wrong side of one fabric rectangle and one fabric circle.

3 SEW THE RECTANGLES TOGETHER TO CREATE A CYLINDER.

Working with the interfaced fabric rectangle, pin together the short edges, interfaced side facing out. Sew together the edges using a ½-inch seam so you have an inside-out cylinder. This will be the outside of the planter. Sew the fabric-only rectangle the same way, also inside out. This will be the inside lining. Press the seams open on both pieces so everything lays flat.

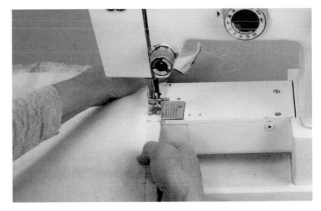

Sew together the short sides of the interfaced rectangle.

Iron the seam open.

Both circles pinned to their respective cylinders.

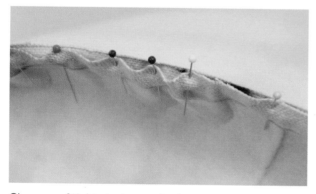

Close-up of tight pinning method.

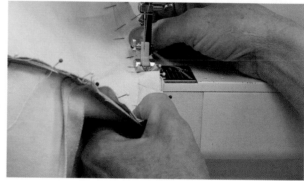

Sew the pinned circular bottom to the cylinder.

4 ATTACH THE BOTTOM.

Pin the interfaced circle to the interfaced cylinder and the fabric-only circle to the fabric-only cylinder. Both pieces should still be inside out. Work the circles into the cylinders by first pinning at four opposite areas and then pinning each quarter. Pin close together and work in the material to minimize puckering.

5 SEW TOGETHER THE CIRCLES AND CYLINDERS.

Sew the pieces together with the bottom of each piece facing up. Go slowly, making sure the cylinder remains flat and away from the needle. When you are finished, you will have two inside-out buckets.

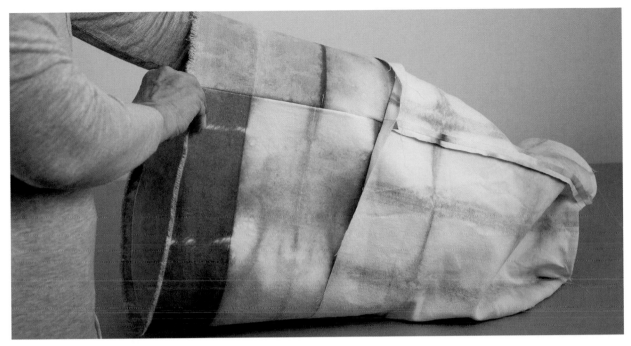

Line up the seams of the nested buckets.

Pin the buckets together, leaving a 5-inch opening.

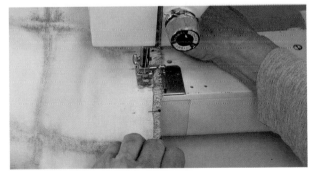

Sew the buckets together, except for the opening.

6 NEST THE INTERFACED BUCKET INTO THE FABRIC BUCKET.

Turn the interfaced bucket right side out. Leave the fabric-only bucket inside out. Nest the interfaced bucket inside the lining bucket. Be sure the seams match up.

7 SEW THE BUCKETS TOGETHER.

Pin the nested buckets together along the top, leaving a 5-inch gap unpinned. Sew the buckets together with a ½-inch seam all along the top, except for the 5-inch opening.

Pull the outer bucket through the hole.

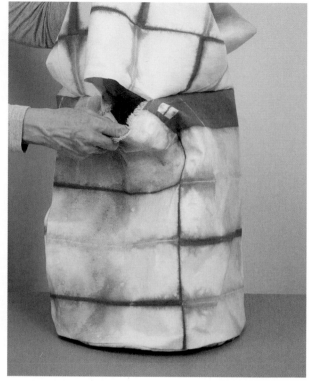
Nest the lining into the outer bucket.

8 PULL THE OUTER BUCKET THROUGH THE OPENING.

Reach your hand into the 5-inch opening and pull the outer bucket (with interfacing) through. It should now be right side out and the lining bucket should push down easily inside it.

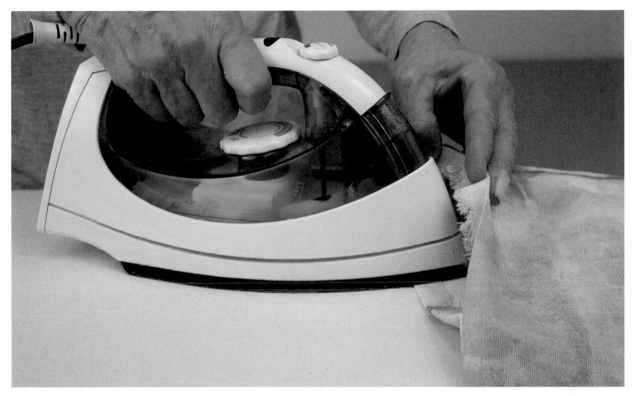

Turn in the edges and iron flat.

9 CLOSE THE GAP AND ADD A TOP STITCH.

On the 5-inch opening that remains, turn in the edges of both the outer and lining buckets to create a ½-inch seam. Iron them flat. Go around the rest of the top edge, ironing everything flat.

When everything is crisp and lying flat, pin together the last opening and sew it all together with a top stitch that circles the entire bucket. You're done! Enjoy making multiple versions of this no-fuss lightweight container for your entire home.

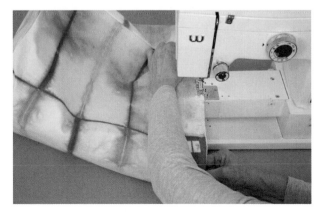

Pin and stitch around the top of the bucket.

A rustic hanging planter floats in midair.

RUSTIC WOOD HANGING PLANTER

Recycle cast-off wood to make a unique hanging planter.

At Potted, we always seem to have little projects or repairs going on. A broken railing, some new shelves, a quick plant stand—these are just some of the jobs we have to tackle. When we are finished, we usually have leftover materials. Over the years we have built up a nice pile of extra wood, but it's never quite enough for a new project, so we end up buying more. But we can't bear to throw away the old stuff. One day we were looking at all those odds and ends and decided to cut them into bits to make hanging planters. It was easy, fast, and a great way to use our extra wood. Our recycling souls were happy.

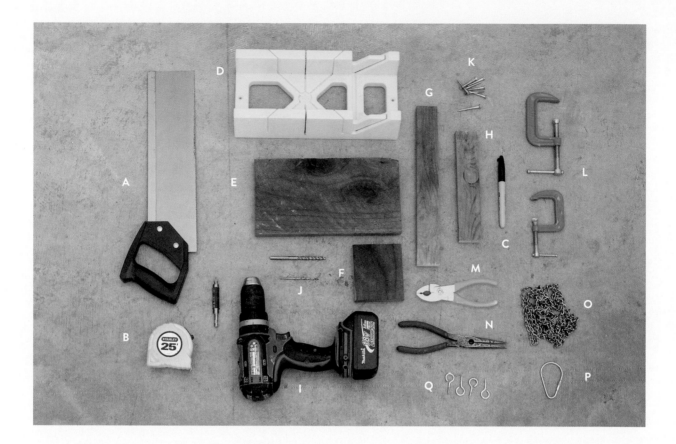

TOOLS & MATERIALS

A. Backsaw

B. Measuring tape

C. Permanent marker

D. Miter box

E. One piece 1 × 6 × 10½-in. wood, for bottom

F. Ten pieces 1 × 4 × 4-in. wood, for sides

G. Two pieces 1 × 2 × 12-in. wood, for long sides of outer frame

H. Two pieces 1 × 2 × 8½-in. wood, for outer frame

I. Drill with Phillips head

J. Drill bits: ¹⁄₁₆-in., for wood predrill; ⅛-in., for eyehook predrill

K. 1¼-in. brass Phillips head #5 screws

L. C clamps

M. Pliers

N. Needle-nose pliers

O. Brass chain

P. Brass carabiner

Q. ¼-in. brass eyehooks

(Hardware can also be stainless steel or any material you prefer.)

PREPARING

If you don't happen to have a pile of wood in your storage area or garage, you can use new wood. The planter requires only short ends, so you may even be able to get free wood. Go to your local building-supply store or lumberyard and check out the area where they cut pieces to order. All sorts of extra bits will be lying around. Ask before you take anything, but we have found that most businesses are happy to turn over any leftovers. You can also check out the dumpsters on construction sites, which are usually filled with small pieces. Wherever you source, look for pieces that are the same thickness. Fencing works great, and old fencing is even better. All wood will eventually start weathering into a beautiful patina, but if you start with old wood, you'll get immediate gratification.

Cut all the wood to length with your backsaw.

1 CUT ALL WOOD PIECES TO SIZE.

Using a measuring tape and marker, follow the materials list to mark all the wood where you will need to cut to size. Cut all the pieces with your miter box and backsaw. If you are making a different size planter than in this project, don't forget to adjust for the actual size of the lumber pieces versus the nominal size (see page 207) and to account for the depth of the wood. A 1-inch side piece will actually be only ¾ inch, so to account for both sides in your overall measurements, subtract 1½ inches (the two side pieces added together) from the desired overall length or width.

Overhead view of all the pieces cut to length.

2 DRILL AND SCREW SIDEPIECES TO BOTTOM.

Lay the bottom piece on a hard, flat surface. Attach the sidepieces one at a time. Predrill holes with the 1/16-inch wood drill bit in the middle of each side panel, then change your bit to a screwdriver head and drill in the screw to secure the piece. One screw per panel is sufficient, as another piece will hold everything together on the outside.

Predrill a hole in the bottom middle of each panel.

Screw the panel in place in the predrilled hole.

View of screwed-in side panels.

Clamp exterior wood frame piece along the middle side of panels to secure it for drilling.

3 ATTACH THE OUTER FRAME.

Use the C clamps to secure each 1 × 2-inch frame piece to the box to keep them from moving around as you attach each piece. Use the same technique as when attaching the sidepieces—predrill one center hole on each piece, and then attach it with a screw.

Measure the center on the wood strip and the center on each panel for drilling the first hole.

Predrill one hole per panel on center.

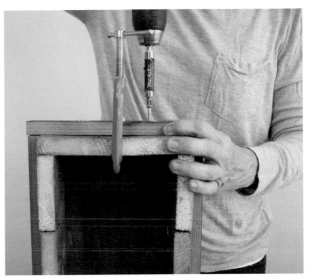

After you have predrilled, screw in all your screws.

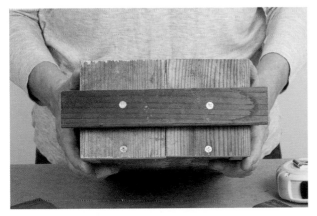

Finished view of short side of rectangle.

Finished view of long side of rectangle.

4 ATTACH THE EYEHOOKS.

To hang the planter, you will need to attach one eyehook in each corner to connect the chain to the planter. Predrill each hole with the ⅛-inch bit, and then screw in the eyehooks by hand. If you bought larger or smaller eyehooks, make sure your predrill bit is smaller so there is enough wood left for the screw to grab on to.

Predrill all four corners with the ⅛-inch drill bit.

> **IF YOU HAVE** a hard time screwing in the eyehooks by hand, try putting a pen or long nail through the eye of the hook and using it as a handle. This will make it much easier to screw in the hook.

Hand screw the eyehooks into the four corners.

5 CONNECT THE CHAIN.

Measure out 12 inches of chain, and use pliers to take it off the longer length. Use standard pliers to hold the link securely, and needle-nose pliers to pull the other side open. Repeat this step until you have four lengths of 12-inch chain (or whatever length you prefer).

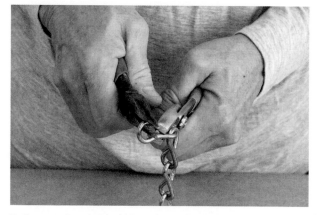

Pull apart the chain until you have four 12-inch lengths.

Attach the chain onto all four corners with the pliers.

A securely attached chain.

Attach the open link to each eyehook, and squeeze it together with the pliers until it is closed and securely attached to the hook.

Finally, close any open links on the other end of each length of chain, and attach all four lengths to the carabiner. Double-check all four lengths to make sure they are the same to ensure the planter hangs evenly. You can use the extra chain to extend the hanging length of the planters; slip it onto the carabiner and it will hang at the top of it. Your planters are now ready to use.

The final planter ready to be hung.

METRIC CONVERSIONS

INCHES	CENTIMETERS
⅓	0.8
½	1.3
¾	1.9
1	2.5
1½	3.8
2	5.0
2½	6.4
3	7.6
4	10.0
5	12.7
6	15.2
7	17.8
8	20.3
9	22.9
10	25.4
12	30.5
14	35.5
15	38.0
18	45.7
20	50.8
24	61.0
28	71.0

FEET	METERS
1	0.3
1½	0.5
2	0.6
3	0.9
4	1.2
5	1.5
6	1.8
7	2.1
8	2.4
9	2.7
10	3.0
12	3.7
15	4.6
20	6.0
30	9.1
40	12.2
50	15.2
70	21.3
80	24.4
100	30.5
130	39.6
5000	1524.0

US VOLUME MEASURE	METRIC EQUIVALENT
$\frac{1}{16}$ teaspoon	0.3 milliliter
$\frac{1}{8}$ teaspoon	0.5 milliliter
$\frac{1}{4}$ teaspoon	1.2 milliliters
$\frac{1}{2}$ teaspoon	2.5 milliliters
1 teaspoon	5.0 milliliters
1 tablespoon (3 teaspoons)	14.8 milliliters
2 tablespoons (1 fluid ounce)	29.6 milliliters
$\frac{1}{8}$ cup (2 tablespoons)	29.6 milliliters
$\frac{1}{4}$ cup (4 tablespoons)	59.1 milliliters
$\frac{1}{2}$ cup (4 fluid ounces)	118.3 milliliters
$\frac{3}{4}$ cup (6 fluid ounces)	177.4 milliliters
1 cup (16 tablespoons)	236.6 milliliters
1 pint (2 cups)	473.2 milliliters
1 quart (4 cups)	946.4 milliliters
1 gallon (16 cups)	3.8 liters

US WEIGHT MEASURE	METRIC EQUIVALENT
$\frac{1}{16}$ ounce	1.8 grams
$\frac{1}{8}$ ounce	3.5 grams
$\frac{1}{4}$ ounce	7.0 grams
$\frac{1}{2}$ ounce	14.2 graams
$\frac{3}{4}$ ounce	21.3 grams
1 ounce	28.3 grams
1$\frac{1}{2}$ ounces	42.5 grams
2 ounces	56.7 grams
3 ounces	85.0 grams
4 ounces	113.4 grams
8 ounces	226.8 grams
10 ounces	283.5 grams
12 ounces	340.2 grams
16 ounces	453.6 grams

ACKNOWLEDGMENTS

This book did not write itself. Timber Press kindly welcomed us, and Juree Sondker and Sarah Milhollin were so helpful and patient with their feedback and support. Many kind and generous people supported us along the way with time, ideas, advice, and very-much-appreciated gardens in which to shoot. We couldn't have done it without your help.

Kim Davis and Chris Wagner, thank you for letting us reshoot the cinderblock wall three times. You know, of course, it was just an excuse to keep hanging out. And Julie Maigret, thanks for pushing us to build the original cinderblock wall.

Sydney Michael and Jonathan Whitehead, we appreciated how many times you let us shoot in your groovy pad. You'll never get rid of us now.

Emily and Larry Karaszewski, thanks for creating such an inspiring home and trusting us to build an unmovable planter in your entry when you weren't even home.

Brett Hofer, we appreciate getting to shoot your Hillside Pottery.

Karen and Guy Vidal, you were our very first project. Thanks for letting us use your amazing tile and being so accommodating.

Meg Brogan and Courtland Cox, thank you for letting us invade your life all those days. It was a really special time—mostly because of Bertie. She will be remembered.

Harriet Fleming and Miguel Sanchez, thanks for trusting us with your patio and giving us free rein to move, build, and paint as we wanted.

Jules Sorenson, your home is as lovely as your heart. We appreciate getting to spend some time there.

Loree Bohl, thanks for the inspiration and permission to use your clever idea—you have so many.

Marisa Frank, you know what it means to be neighborly, and we appreciated your lovely home so much.

Lorraine and Ric Heitzman, thanks for being so accommodating. True friends, indeed.

Teresa Grow, thank you for letting us rummage through your recycling bins to find the perfect piece of wallpaper. The project wouldn't have worked without it.

Thomas Zamora and Paul Rojas, thank you for generously giving us free rein in your yard. May the force be with you.

Joy and Roland Feuer, thanks for creating the mecca that is Mt. Feuer and letting us shoot there. So glad you walked into our store all those years ago.

Finally thanks to our families, Gustavo and Lola Gutierrez and Max and Zane Gray Wilbur. They put up with our DIY obsession and reminded us to breathe.

This fabric bucket planter can be made to match any decor style.

FURTHER READING

These books are inspirational, and many helped us learn construction techniques. Some are dated, but they offer the same spark to the imagination as when they were brand new. We hope they will help if you want to delve a little deeper into your own designs.

Beverley, Deena. *Tiling and Mosaics in a Weekend.* Cincinnati, OH: Betterway Books, 2002.

Blakeney, Justina. *The New Bohemians.* New York, NY: Abrams, 2015.

Brown, Jane. *The Modern Garden.* New York, NY: Princeton Architectural Press, 2000.

Cole, Rebecca. *Paradise Found: Gardening in Unlikely Places.* New York, NY: Clarkson Potter Publishers, 2000.

Corwin, Lena. *Made by Hand.* New York, NY: Abrams, 2013.

Edwards Forkner, Lorene. *Handmade Garden Projects.* Portland, OR: Timber Press, 2011.

Heibel, Tara, and Tassy de Give. *Rooted in Design.* Berkeley, CA: Ten Speed Press, 2015.

Maurer-Mathison, Diane. *The Ultimate Marbling Handbook.* New York, NY: Watson-Guptill Publications, 1999.

Nilsson, Malin, and Camilla Arvidsson. *Concrete Garden Projects.* Portland, OR: Timber Press, 2012.

Oppenheimer, Betty. *Sew & Stow.* North Adams, MA: Storey Publishing, 2008.

Palmisano, Joanne. *Salvage Secrets Design & Decor.* New York, NY: W.W. Norton & Company, 2014.

Sabo Wills, Margaret. *Decorating with Tile.* Upper Saddle River, NJ: Creative Homeowner Press, 2000.

Sanders, Charles A. *The PVC Project Book.* Short Hills, NJ: Burford Books, Inc., 2005.

Shotwell, Robyn E., ed., and the editors of Sunset Books and Sunset Magazine. *Plant Containers You Can Make.* Menlo Park, CA: Lane Publishing Co., 1977.

Skote, Malena. *Easy Concrete.* New York, NY: Lark Books, 2009.

Vejar, Kristine. *The Modern Natural Dyer.* New York, NY: Stewart, Tabori & Chang, 2015.

Voegele, Christoph. *Sophie Taeuber-Arp Works on Paper.* Heidelberg, Germany: Kehrer Verlag, 2003.

RESOURCES

You can easily find the materials for the projects in this book locally or online. We frequented the home-improvement stores Home Depot and Lowe's because they are readily available almost everywhere, but we highly recommend exploring your local hardware and art-supply stores as much as possible. Not only will you be supporting your neighborhood small businesses, but you also have a better chance of getting valuable insights and help from the knowledgeable people who work there.

Regional building materials yards are also a treasure trove of DIY finds. These yards have a more specific purpose, but you can find a wealth of materials just by walking around and reimagining their purpose, as we did for many of the projects in this book. Another customer may have refused special-order items that you could pick up for a song. The yard might make its own design for concrete blocks that sets your imagination on fire. Imagine home-improvement stores as the department stores of materials and building yards as the boutiques.

Yard sales, flea markets, and salvage yards are also good sources of materials and inspiration. It's fun to browse and let yourself be open to what you may find.

Following is a list of suppliers we used to source the projects for this book:

BLICK ART SUPPLIES

www.dickblick.com

Art-supply stores carrying a great selection of Testors paint, which is used in Marbleized Masterpieces.

CHERRY CREEK COTTAGE

www.cherrycreekcottage.com

This online vendor offers a great selection of Crow Canyon Home enamelware, which is used in Kitchen Confidential.

DESIGN VIDAL

www.designvidal.com

Design Vidal is a bicoastal home design firm that created the tiles used in Cement Tile Custom Container. You can purchase tile via the website, but minimums do apply.

DHARMA TRADING COMPANY

www.dharmatrading.com

Supplies materials for dyeing fabric, as with shibori for Fabric Bucket. The site is also a valuable resource if you want to learn more about dyeing fabric.

GLOBAL INDUSTRIAL

www.globalindustrial.com

While local livestock feed and supply stores are the best source for purchasing stock tanks (as for Stock Tank Water Garden), you can also find them on this website.

GRAHAM & BROWN

www.grahambrown.com

An international resource for wallpaper. Look for End of Line vaues for small quantities.

GRANADA TILE

www.granadatile.com

This company produces cement tile, and you can purchase tiles and samples online.

HABITAT FOR HUMANITY

www.habitat.org

Consult their website to find a local ReStore near you to purchase used and surplus building supplies at a fraction of the cost. All proceeds help fund the construction of Habitat for Humanity houses in local communities.

HEATH CERAMICS

www.heathceramics.com

We used Heath tile for Tiled Cinderblock Planter. Although Heath has fairly large minimum requirements for purchase, you can buy samples online or in the San Francisco or Los Angeles stores.

HOME DEPOT

www.homedepot.com

Home-improvement stores throughout North America. Many items are also available for online purchase.

JO-ANN'S

www.joann.com

Fabric and crafting stores located throughout North America and online. Look for online coupons for additional savings.

LOWE'S

www.lowes.com

Home-improvement stores throughout North America. Many items are also available for online purchase.

MADISON AND GROW

www.madisonandgrow.com

The Los Angeles–based wallpaper company we used for Decoupage Goes Outdoors.

MICHAEL'S CRAFT STORES

www.michaels.com

Craft-supply stores throughout the United States and Canada. Good selection of stencils, paints, and general arts and crafts supplies.

MODWALLS

www.modwalls.com

Good source for ceramic and glass tile for Tiled Cinderblock Planter. You can purchase samples or try the Outlet section, which features discounted items in smaller quantities.

TRUE VALUE HARDWARE STORES

www.truevalue.com

National network of locally owned hardware stores. Most try to maintain the helpful customer service that larger chains cannot always provide.

TUNDRA RESTAURANT SUPPLY

www.etundra.com

Restaurant-supply company that sells the inexpensive stainless steel salad bowls we used for Flying Saucer Planters.

PHOTO CREDITS

INDEX

Testors Enamel Model Paint, 156
Thimaporn, Pawena, 165
thrill-fill-spill planting method, 145
tile
    cutting, 12
    designing with, 38, 41
    measuring, 41
    in projects, 34–43, 52–59
tools, 12–13. *See also project lists; specific tools*
trailing foliage, 85
trees, small, 39, 70, 181, 194

underplantings, 134
utility knife, 12

vent cover wall planter, 60, 78–85
vertical gardens
    privacy screen, 86–95
    vent cover wall planters, 60, 78–85
vincas, 25
violas, 62

wallpaper, 175–177
wallpapered planter, 174–181
wall planters, 60, 78–85, 122–131
water features, 117
water garden, 106, 117–121
weeping fig, 181
wire cutters, 13
wire hangers, 112–113, 143–145
wire rope, 140
wiring together PVC tubes, 74, 76–77

ANNETTE GOLITI GUTIERREZ and **MARY GRAY** met many years ago during their former lives in the film industry. Mary was a set decorator and art director for commercials and television. Annette was a screenwriter and ad-agency producer whose true passion was remodeling houses. With no retail experience, they bought a run-down pottery store, which over the course of a decade they built into Potted, an outdoor-lifestyle destination and brand. Their love of plants took them down a path to creating their own distinctive containers.

Annette does the marketing for Potted, as well as garden design work. She writes a blog for pottedstore.com, and also contributes to the blog for Sunset Magazine. Mary is the principal buyer and head of visuals at Potted. She seeks out local artisans and global treasures, which come together as Potted style.

Their work has been featured in the *LA Times*, *Sunset Magazine*, *Los Angeles Magazine Best Of*, *California Home + Design*, and *Country Living*, as well as on websites including Gardenista, Apartment Therapy, Design Sponge, Garden Design, and the Huffington Post. They participate annually in the Dwell on Design event in Los Angeles, and are frequently mentioned in "Best of" roundups.